The European Debt Crisis

João Moreira Rato

The European Debt Crisis

How Portugal Navigated the post-2008 Financial Crisis

palgrave
macmillan

João Moreira Rato
NOVA IMS
Universidade Nova de Lisboa
Lisbon, Portugal

ISBN 978-3-030-61173-6 ISBN 978-3-030-61174-3 (eBook)
https://doi.org/10.1007/978-3-030-61174-3

This Palgrave Macmillan imprint is published by the registered company Springer Nature Switzerland AG.
The registered company address is: Gewerbestrasse 11, 6330 Cham, Switzerland

To Inês and to my sons, Francisco and Luís, for their constant support and patience

CHAPTER 1

Background

Abstract This chapter describes the economic situation in Portugal following the Global Financial Crisis. Flows coming from the European Central Bank via the Target 2 system enabled Portugal to keep twin deficits in its external and fiscal accounts. It allowed Portugal to continue accumulating domestic and external debt. This accumulation of debt and the negative evolution of the European government bond market conditions led Portugal to request financial assistance from the Troika in April 2011. In doing so, it was following Ireland and Greece, which had requested assistance in 2010. The assistance program was designed with the aim of stabilizing both public and external debt flows. During the first year of the program, the new government managed to stabilize the macroeconomic situation. But during the same period, discussions around a second program for Greece introduced the possibility of private bondholders haircuts in Europe. This possibility originated a succession of negative sovereign rating reactions and government bond prices in the periphery to get to more distressed levels. In this context, I explain what my motivation was to join the Debt Management Office. My mission was to design and implement a plan to re-establish market access for Portuguese government bonds.

Keywords Troika • European debt crisis • Greek PSI • Euro redenomination risk • Portuguese assistance program • Global Financial Crisis

J. M. Rato, *The European Debt Crisis*,
https://doi.org/10.1007/978-3-030-61174-3_1

During the first decade of the twenty-first century, in the happy days preceding the Global Financial Crisis, Portugal had been spending beyond its means. It had been accumulating a high stock of debt vis-à-vis external borrowers. Foreign banks, insurance companies, asset managers and multilateral institutions like the European Investment Bank ("EIB") had been accumulating Portuguese private and public debt. The Portuguese economy was depending on external credit to guarantee a certain level of domestic economic growth. Portuguese households were buying their houses with recourse to foreign money. Home ownership increased at a rapid pace. Local banks would aggressively finance mortgages, repackaging them into securitization vehicles; the vehicles would then issue bonds and those bonds were then placed with international investors. The banks were also active in financing corporations, a good share of which either were developers or offered real estate as collateral for their borrowings. The banks were financing the gap between credit and deposits by issuing bonds they would then sell in the international markets. Portugal's economic growth was meek when compared with other Eurozone countries but even these modest levels of growth were being sustained by external investors in Portuguese bonds and loans. These bonds took different names: mortgage-backed securities, SME securitization bonds, senior bank bonds, subordinated bank bonds, Portuguese government bonds. A good share of these bonds were originated by the domestic banking sector and then placed abroad with the assistance of global investment banks. The Portuguese banks had the highest share of credit not financed by deposits in Europe. To finance the difference they came regularly to the international markets with bond offerings; some of these bond programs took specific domestic names, like the name of a Portuguese horse breed or the name of Portuguese navigators like Magellan. As in Hollywood blockbusters, they were issued in series, I, II, III, IV and so on.

In parallel, public sector corporations were financing a good share of their capital expenditures with recourse to external lenders that were banking on the Portuguese State's implicit guarantee. The railways, the subway companies, counted on loans from the EIB but also from some foreign banks specialized in public sector loans, like Dexia and Depfa, to keep their investment levels. Roads were being built with borrowed money originating in the same sources. By 2016, and following the building program preceding 2011, Portugal's quality of road infrastructure was classified by the World Economic Forum as the ninth best in the world, just ahead of Denmark, Taiwan and Finland.

Portugal had been accumulating external deficits since the second half of the 1990s but these accelerated with the turn of the century. This, of course, came in tandem with the accumulation of private credit financed by foreign investors. As a consequence, external debt kept accumulating. The economy was addicted to these private external sources of funds. Households needed them to keep consuming, corporations to finance their new projects, and in some cases to cover their persistent losses, and public sector companies to keep investing and building more roads.

In 2003, the government tried to engineer a slowdown but with growth already quite fragile, it did not persist in its effort. So when the 2008 financial crisis ("the Global Financial Crisis") closed some of the private bond and loan markets that the Portuguese banks were using, Portugal ran the risk of being forced into an uncontrolled adjustment that could derail the economy very sharply. Without the availability of external financing sources, imports would have to contract markedly causing a possibly catastrophic adjustment in domestic consumption and investment.

Luckily for the government of the time, the government bond market remained open and the European Central Bank ("ECB") started to play a bigger role in the European financial markets. As the financing of domestic banks by external private investors decreased sharply, the financing of the Portuguese external deficits started to rely on the Target 2 balances at the ECB, central bank credits that replaced private flows from surplus countries toward deficit countries. These funds from the ECB counterbalanced the reduction in external private financing of the domestic banking sector. They kept the external financing flowing: as a measure of external dependence, the Portuguese current account deficit reached its peak in 2008. This allowed the Portuguese economy just to muddle through in 2008, with an almost flat economic growth as the access to foreign funds was maintained. As we have seen, these flows were now different in their composition. In 2009 the Portuguese economy was contracting almost by 3% but by 2010 it was already experiencing 1.9% growth. How was this recovery possible given the circumstances?

Given the importance of the role that the Target 2 system played in keeping external funding to the Portuguese economy after the Global Financial Crisis, I will try to explain how the system works in a simple way. Consider a Portuguese corporate that wants to acquire a new fleet of Volkswagens from Germany. The corporate will ask its bank in Portugal to make a transfer to Volkswagen's bank in Germany to process the payment implied by this transaction. Both banks have accounts in their respective central banks. The Portuguese bank submits the payment instructions to Target 2. The Portuguese bank account will show a debit in the system and the German bank account will show, symmetrically, a credit. As a result of this transaction, the Bank of Portugal will generate a liability to the ECB and the Bundesbank a credit to the ECB. Target 2 balances represent the aggregate difference of these debits and credits between national central banks all over Europe. A country like Portugal that continued to accumulate external deficits, exporting less than it imports, and given these deficits were no longer financed by private flows, would accumulate negative balances in the Target 2 system. After 2008, external deficits of European peripheral countries like Portugal were financed by central bank funding. The National Central Bank was financed through Target 2 by the central banks of countries that had external surpluses like Germany and the Netherlands. After 2009, private flows toward deficit countries had dried out and were actually flowing to safe havens like Germany. Anyway, this system allowed Portugal to continue to accumulate external deficits after the Global Financial Crisis. These were only corrected after the country followed the economic and financial adjustment measures prescribed by the Troika.[1] As you may expect, in case you do not remember the public debate at the time, Target 2 balances created some discomfort for the authorities in the surplus countries, even if the matter was too technical to be understood by the majority of the public opinion. The system allowed deficit countries to avoid a deep adjustment in their domestic consumption and investment patterns.

To keep the economy from contracting further following the 2009 crisis and to stabilize it in 2010, the Portuguese government decided, at the time, to increase expenditures and embark in record budget deficits; 2009 saw a big increase in government expenditures as a percentage of GDP after a few years of contraction and a small increase in 2008. These policies culminated in record government deficits in 2009 and 2010. They were intended to compensate for the impact in the contraction of private credit growth coming from the higher prudence on the part of the banks, for

[1] Troika: name given to the group of three institutions involved in the design and monitoring of the assistance programs in Europe during the peripheral debt crisis. The group consisted of the International Monetary Fund ("IMF"), the European Commission and the ECB.

Foreword

Greece looms large in the perception of the European debt crisis, with Athens the natural focal point of attention. Yet it was far from the only country to find itself against the ropes in a multi-faceted, multi-pronged and existential crisis for the common currency project. Portugal was often the forgotten front, but its success in navigating the tumultuous period was no less important. João Moreira Rato's detailed exploration of how Portugal found itself in dire straits, how it navigated the mess and ultimately managed to slowly rebuild investor confidence regain access to international capital markets in 2013 is therefore a vital contribution to the ongoing post-mortem of the European debt crisis—with lessons we can all learn from.

Global Finance Correspondent, *Financial Times* Robin Wigglesworth

Contents

which their usual financing sources had dried. This kept the economy going, surviving the threat of a sharp contraction, as the government and the public sector companies engineered more spending, with the corresponding external deficits financed by the Target 2 system.

As a consequence of these policies, direct government debt increased during the period due to the accumulation of deficits. In addition, the State accumulated debt outside of the direct public debt perimeter through public sector companies, as a good share of them were loss making. During this period, the government embarked on a massive school building program and continued to build roads and tunnels. From 2007, before the financial crisis, to 2010, the public debt in percentage of GDP increased by more than 35 percentage points.

As expected, the market conditions in which this debt was placed were getting worse and worse, in a process that mimicked what happened with other peripheral Europe sovereigns following the Global Financial Crisis. After the disclosure of a massive budget deficit in 2009, Greece had requested support from the Troika in April 2010. In the meantime, Ireland, suffering from the aftershocks of the Global Financial Crisis and its impact on the banks, saw a massive accumulation in public debt and had to ask for external support from the Troika in November 2010. The yields on Portuguese government bonds, or the interest the State had to pay annually to investors on freshly issued bonds, started 2010 close to 4% but ended the year close to 7%. The fact that rating agencies started to reduce the rating attached to these sovereign bonds did not help.

In early January 2009, Portugal was considered a AA quality by the three most widely used rating agencies, Moody's, Fitch and S&P, close to the current rating notation for France. During that month, S&P downgraded Portugal to A+ and in March 2011 to BBB-, just above investment grade. Below investment grade, the rating is considered speculative grade, and a proportion of buy and hold institutional investors in government bonds, like insurance companies, pension funds and more conservative mutual funds, become constrained by their own investment rules, in their capacity to hold the bonds in the portfolios. Potentially, there will be a lot of forced sellers of the bonds at that point. Some of these constraints on investors' capacity to hold speculative grade bonds depend on at least two rating agencies. In consequence, most investors become forced sellers when two agencies downgrade the sovereign from investment grade to speculative grade, although they may start selling in anticipation.

Moody's downgraded Portugal to A1 in July 2010 and then closer to speculative grade in April 2011, Baa1 (Baa3 is the last rating in investment grade). And Fitch downgraded Portugal to A+ in December 2010, just before Christmas, and then to BBB- on 1 April 2011.[2] So, from 2009 to 2011, when Portugal had to request for assistance from the Troika, a gradual but sustained process of rating downgrades was taking place. It became clear that the rating agencies' perception of the Portuguese government's credit quality was decreasing.

During the previous decade, Portuguese government bonds had been sold to investors located in Europe, to French, German and UK institutions including banks, asset managers and insurance companies. The latter would buy these bonds and hold them in their books. The Portuguese investors represented, generally, only around 10–20% of investment in new Portuguese government bonds.

This started to change in 2010. In February 2011, the Treasury and Debt Management Office for Portugal ("IGCP"), which had the responsibility to execute the issuance of new bonds, came to the market with a new five-year bond. This bond offered a coupon of 6.4%. As it was sold at a discount, the yield on the bond was even a bit higher (6.46% in reality). This level of annual interest, paid to investors by a country with a level of debt expected to cross 100% of GDP during that same year and with a clear positive public debt trend, worried most investors. The fact that Portugal was willing to pay a yield of that magnitude to investors was perceived as a sign of despair given the circumstances. It showed that the need was there to keep going to the market whatever the conditions. And as we will see later, it is never good to make it clear to investors that you really need market support to survive. This effect was re-enforced given the sovereign was on a negative path in terms of debt accumulation and given adverse external market circumstances. Keep in mind that by the beginning of 2011 investors had already seen a similar process unfolding in Greece and Ireland. Both countries had been through a process of increasing public debt and deteriorating market conditions and both processes culminated with the need for external public support.

[2] Rating agencies attribute grades to issuers according to their views of their credit quality, based on quantitative and subjective criteria. The highest quality starts at AAA for S&P and Fitch and Aaa for Moody's and decreases to AA+ and Aa1 and then all the way to C if the issuer has not defaulted in its obligations.

In addition to the issuance of Portuguese government bonds with a remaining life of more than one year, the Portuguese Treasury issues Treasury Bills that mature in less than one year. At the beginning of 2011, these bills were placed mostly with Portuguese banks. Domestic banks would bring the bills to the ECB as collateral for funding. Even so, the cost of these very short term instruments increased substantially: from an average of 1.6% in 2010 to 4.9% in 2011 for three-month Treasury Bills. It became clear that the banks had less and less capacity to absorb the needs of the Portuguese Treasury.

Market closure, which meant that international investors were no longer willing to buy new issuances of Portuguese government bonds whatever their maturities,[3] was hovering on the horizon. In these circumstances, Portugal would only be able to issue very short bonds (three months, six months) and only to domestic investors. These bonds are normally kept for liquidity reasons, a way to invest balances that need to be easily converted into cash to honor short-term commitments besides being used as collateral for funding from the ECB. Domestic banks, at the time, would take these bonds and finance them at the ECB and keep the difference between the cost of funds and the yield on the bonds. When that was the case, the ECB would be indirectly financing the Portuguese government. As expected, the ECB was not willing to do that indefinitely. If that was going to be the case, they preferred to contact the authorities and advise them to ask for a formal support program like the Irish and the Greeks had done before. As a consequence, the incapacity to issue bonds with maturities higher than one year was pushing the Portuguese government into a corner. The government, to refinance the existing bonds and to pay for its budget deficits, had to look for alternative sources of funding: the Troika was the available candidate. The domestic banks could have been an alternative, up to a certain point, but, as seen above, they were still dealing with a process of reducing their investments following the Global Financial Crisis and had limited capacity to invest in medium to long term government bonds. Actually, there are multiple indications that they were reaching capacity and it was under their recommendation that the Minister of Finance eventually advised the Prime Minister to ask for the Troika' s support following the footsteps of Ireland and Greece.

[3] The cash notional, or reference amount on the bond, is repaid at maturity.

On 7 April 2011, the Portuguese government requested for assistance from the Troika.

To add fuel to the fire, the budget deficit for 2010, which was initially expected to come at a very high value of 7.3% of GDP, the target agreed with the European Commission, was corrected to an even higher value of 9.1% on 23 April. This process reminded investors of the Greek situation. Greece had experienced, during 2010, massive corrections of its 2009 budget deficit number.[4] These corrections contributed to an increase in market stress for Greek bonds, as investors lost any confidence in the Greek statistics and in their capacity to provide a truthful picture of the domestic situation. In addition, in the case of Portugal, part of the upward revisions were due to sensitive happenings at the time: banking sector recapitalizations and reclassifications within public expenditure of public sector and Public Private Partnerships ("PPPs"), including ones linked to road expenditure. Investors worried, when confronted with these corrections, about two things: lack of transparency in public accounts that could bring more surprises to the forefront and lack of control in public expenditure. They had seen it before in other places: reclassification of debts and expenditures within the State, correcting for past questionable accounting practices and financial sector liabilities taken over by the central government.

On 7 May, the economic and financial assistance program was agreed at a technical level between the Troika and the Portuguese authorities.

When designing the program, as was the case in multiple previous programs, the lenders are interested in creating the conditions to minimize the period for which the country under assistance requires funding. They expect the borrower to be capable of raising funds on its own when the program ends. For this to happen, you need the borrower to be able to repay its bonds and to finance all budgetary needs (and other needs that may arise outside of the budget as, for example, bank recapitalization), with recourse to the market. That is why a robust sovereign bond market recovery is so important, for which it is crucial for the country to stabilize its external accounts such as to regain the interest of external private investors. As mentioned previously, the countries from Northern Europe were not comfortable at the time with the accumulation of Target 2 liabilities by the countries in the European periphery. Portugal had a dual problem:

[4] The Greek government deficit was also revised upward in 2010 in what concerned the years 2006–2008.

a high and growing stock of external debt and a high and growing stock of public debt. To deal with both, the program had to be designed to decrease both deficits, external and public, to induce a slowdown in the accumulation of public and external debt and to eventually set the country in the direction of sustained debt reduction.

With these objectives in mind, the program was structured around three pillars: balanced fiscal consolidation, frontloaded structural reforms and financial sector stabilization. The third one was crucial to ensure that State intervention in the banks would be limited and would not weigh disorderly on public expenditure and public debt. The second one aimed at strengthening the competitiveness of the Portuguese economy and corporate productivity, to boost exports and correct long-term trade imbalances. Plainly, the program targeted budget deficits (there are explicit quantitative targets in the program) and external funding needs. Note that on the third pillar the program mentioned the aim of re-opening access to interbank and bond markets for banks. If successful, Portugal could decrease its use of funding coming from the ECB.

The program size was €78 billion, with one-third coming from the IMF and two-thirds from the European Union. As is usual in these programs, the cash would be delivered in tranches: €38 billion in 2011, €25 billion in 2012, €10 billion in 2013, €5 billion in 2014. The financing included the full repayment for all the bonds up to June 2013. From then on, market access was expected.

Following the program's announcement, things got worse before they got better. The prices of the Portuguese government bonds underwent a more prolonged period of depreciation up to the start of 2012. The annual yield demanded by investors to buy a five-year Portuguese government bond in the secondary market went over 20% in January 2012. Remember how this compares with close to 6.4% for the five-year bonds issued in February 2011!

The market underperformance was partly due to a change in paradigm in Europe. Following the negative performance of the Greek program, as Greece seemed to have fallen into a negative economic spiral, the need for a second bailout was becoming evident. In Greece, a deeper recession was increasing the sovereign's financing needs, as tax revenues suffered and social contributions grew as a consequence of the higher rhythm of domestic economy contraction. These ever growing financing needs demanded more financial support from the Troika. As part of this second program, European authorities were pushing for a haircut on private sector holdings of bonds. This haircut could be close to 50%. It presented investors with a new situation: for the first time European officials accepted that losses on the bonds of a Eurozone sovereign were possible. The haircut on bonds held by private sector investors was called Private Sector Involvement ("PSI"). The theme had been introduced by Schauble on 6 June 2011.[5]

The question was if more members of the Eurozone would have to follow this precedent. And, as it seemed that the recipe that was being used in Greece was not working, where would it end? If the Greek program had no solution following an haircut to private sector holdings of bonds, would there be a need for the public sector, the ECB and other Eurozone and European Union countries to take some losses too? If the latter proved impossible for political reasons and/or the economy failed to stabilize, would Greece have to leave the euro and start using a new currency to allow for an economic adjustment? If that was going to be the case, would it be the only country to have to do so? This generated a new perception of risk for investors: redenomination risk, the risk that an asset in euros is redenominated in a new currency with less value for the investor. This risk seems to have shown up in Europe in 2011 and peaked in the summer of 2012 when Mario Draghi made a speech promising that the ECB would do "whatever it takes" to ensure the integrity of the euro.[6]

Portuguese sovereign bonds suffered, as in parallel the Big 3 rating agencies pushed Portugal to below investment grade. Moody's was the first mover on 5 July 2011, bringing Portugal's rating to Ba2 (below Ba3, the highest quality rating within the junk status). Fitch followed, pushing Portugal to BB+ on 21 November; later came S&P, attributing to Portugal a BB rating on 13 January 2012. But, as explained before, the real limitations for most investors arise when there are two or more downgrades. Then they will be forced to sell the bonds according to their investment rules. But the first downgrade can also be read as a signal that more downgrades from the other rating agencies are to be expected. When you consider the justification for the first of these downgrades, the one effected by Moody's, you can sense the impact that the Greek situation, notably the discussions around the Greek PSI, was having on Portugal:

[5]For a chronology, check "The Greek debt restructuring: an autopsy" by Zettelmeyer, Trebesch and Gulati.

[6]Check Roberto De Santis, "A measure of redenomination risk", ECB Working Paper Series, April 2015.

The following drivers prompted Moody's decision to downgrade and assign a negative outlook:

1. The growing risk that Portugal will require a second round of official financing before it can return to the private market, and the increasing possibility that private sector creditor participation will be required as a pre-condition.
2. Heightened concerns that Portugal will not be able to fully achieve the deficit reduction and debt stabilization targets set out in its loan agreement with the European Union (EU) and International Monetary Fund (IMF) due to the formidable challenges the country is facing in reducing spending, increasing tax compliance, achieving economic growth and supporting the banking system.[7]

The same press release stated: "it is the increasing probability that Portugal will not be able to borrow at sustainable rates in the capital markets in the second half of 2013," which was a pre-condition for the assistance program to be agreed, and was one of the drivers for this decision. And, in case that risk becomes real, given what was happening in Greece, Moody's was expecting that private investors would have to be called in. According to Moody's, this new precedent generated by the Greek PSI "is significant not only because it increases the economic risks facing current investors, but also because it may discourage new private sector lending going forward and reduces the likelihood that Portugal will soon be able to regain market access on sustainable terms."

As the negotiations surrounding the voluntary losses to be taken by banks, insurance companies and other private sector investors, which were fundamental for Greece to achieve a second bailout, dragged, S&P took the decision to downgrade simultaneously the rating of nine Eurozone countries including Portugal. S&P stated: "today's rating actions are primarily driven by our assessment that the policy initiatives that have been taken by European policymakers in recent weeks may be insufficient to fully address ongoing systemic stresses in the eurozone."[8] As part of this rating action, France was stripped for the first time of its AAA rating by S&P. The rating agency justified its concerns by expressing its doubts that

[7] Moody's investor service press release for the rating action taken on 5 July 2011.

[8] S&P 14 January press release as reported by Reuters on 14 January in Business News, "S&P downgrades nine euro zone countries".

Eurozone countries would be able to agree on a plan with enough firepower to deal with the Eurozone's existing financial issues.

Following the S&P decision of January 2012, on 13 February, in another round of simultaneous downgrades involving multiple Eurozone countries and justified by continued policy uncertainty in Europe, Moody's downgraded Portugal to Ba3, closing the cycle of downgrades for the Portuguese sovereign. In its decision Moody's mentions as a driver "the increased likelihood of a disorderly default by Greece (...) [which] will very likely make Portugal unable to access long-term market funding in September 2013 as planned, and increase pressure on the government to seek a debt restructuring."[9] These rating decisions increased the downward pressure on the prices at which the Portuguese ten-year bonds were exchanging hands in the secondary market (where already existing bonds transact), which experienced its bottom in February 2012. The annual yield differential to the German government bonds (Bunds) yield came close to a 15% differential. Investors needed to receive a premium of close to 15% a year to invest on a ten-year Portuguese Bond instead of a German one. And both countries were part of the same single currency area!

By February 2012, I was living in London and watching these events unfold from a distance. Following a PhD in economics at the University of Chicago, with a thesis in financial economics completed in 2000, I had, like many of my colleagues at the time, decided to pursue a career in finance, more specifically in fixed income, in London. Fixed income deals with the markets for bonds and with interest rates, as opposed to equities. In general, banks included fixed income, commodities and currencies in the same division. With our PhDs under our arms, we had a lot of demand to work in derivatives, which was an area within fixed income (and also but to a lesser extent in equities), that was growing. It was starting to take over the classic areas linked to plain vanilla bonds as the main source of revenues in fixed income for investment banks. Derivatives allowed users the flexibility to adapt to different investment profiles and for clients to protect against different types of risks arising from any specific contingencies. Since 2000, I had been working in different US investment banks and in different client-facing roles. I knew how to communicate with investors, investment banks and other market players. In addition, my economics PhD allowed me to read the macroeconomic information and understand

[9] Moody's press release of 13 February, "Moody's adjusts ratings of 9 European sovereigns to capture downside risks."

its dynamics. Throughout my years in London, and even during my years in Chicago, I had kept in the back of my mind a fascination with economic policy and an intention to do public service for my country at a given stage in my career.

At the start of 2012, I could understand the importance for Portugal of regaining market access and how this was a crucial component of the adjustment program. It was obvious at the time that for this objective to be achieved, the Portuguese authorities had to reverse the negative market perceptions that were only strengthened by the latest rating agencies' reviews. As we will see throughout the book, these perceptions quickly become self-fulfilling. If investors avoid your bonds fearing your incapacity to re-establish market access, how will you obtain the funds that will make a second Troika bailout program unnecessary? Very quickly, that incapacity becomes a reality and you will need further Troika support. That was what was happening in the market for Portuguese bonds at the time: a buyers strike that made it impossible to issue new bonds to finance upcoming bond redemptions, deficits and the surprises still coming out of the banking sector, public sector companies and PPPs. This buyers strike had been deepened by the Greek PSI spillovers and the rating agencies' downgrades. These downgrades created a lot of forced selling of the bonds. In addition, at the time, there was a heightened sensitivity on the part of bank and insurance companies shareholders regarding their exposure to the bonds of the European periphery. These exposure numbers started being published regularly by some of the banks and there was pressure on these financial institutions to show that this exposure was decreasing. Given the absence of buyers, this reduction in bond holdings was not easy to achieve and, as we have seen, the prices of the bonds plummeted to new lows.

I could also see two other processes taking place. The Troika program was proving successful in Portugal in reducing the negative flows both in the external and in the fiscal accounts. The second one was the lack of trust that existed on the part of the government in the existing IGCP leadership that was inherited from the previous government.

The government had been able to achieve a very strong adjustment in the government budget deficit at the start of the program and the external accounts reacted in a spectacular way bringing the external balances very close to equilibrium in a very short period of time. The program had been clearly frontloaded in an economic textbook fashion. This is normally important for an adjustment program to succeed. The highest pain for the population comes at the start and then allows for the situation to improve later on, decreasing the risks of making the program socially and politically unsustainable. At the same time, it allows for the results of the efforts to be perceived quickly by potential investors. Those investors will play a crucial role in the process of re-establishing bond issuance and on the creation of a virtuous circle in the bond markets. If the negative flows start to reverse, the external and government deficits start showing a strong decrease and investors will start coming back into bond markets anticipating a future debt reduction momentum. Additionally, the first quarter of 2012 GDP growth numbers came in (negative at the time obviously), showing that the pace of economic contraction was decreasing when compared with the previous two quarters. This could be perceived as a signal that the economy was not entering a vicious circle similar to the one that had been experienced by Greece.

On the other hand, the IGCP leadership had been very involved in marketing the last bonds that had been sold into the market and for that reason could lack some credibility. The existing Ministry of Finance was therefore not willing to allow them to start contacting investors because it thought the timing was not right as it was keen to build up credibility before re-engaging with investors. Further, by the second quarter of 2012, when the Ministry of Finance was starting to become comfortable with the results of the adjustment process, it was clear that it was not happy to have the old IGCP team communicating to the market players about the situation in Portugal and the path that was to be followed from there.

I could see this clearly. And the conviction that this could be the opportunity to participate in a unique historical process in my country and to contribute with my expertise for public service was growing within me. I believed this challenge was well consistent with my skill set: I knew how to read the fixed income markets, to communicate with market players, to structure and execute transactions. It was my turn to give something back. My country had given me support in the past, with scholarships when I was at the University of Chicago. So, after 17 years outside of Portugal, my wife and I decided that the time was right to come back.

With this conviction, I called a friend of mine that I knew was very close to the Prime Minister. I knew the current Prime Minister from collaborations in brainstorming sessions before the election. I explained my idea to this good friend. It was clear that the IGCP was lacking leadership at an important juncture and I could be the right person to do the job. He agreed with me and promised he would mention it to the Prime Minister.

This conversation took place on a weekend. By the start of the week, my friend called me back with the number of an assistant to contact in view of setting up a meeting with the Prime Minister. We set up a meeting for the following Friday at the end of the day in the Prime Minister's residence.

On a cold winter Friday evening, in early 2012, I was waiting to be received in a big room where Prime Ministers receive guests, looking out of the window into the darkness of the garden. I had a strange feeling that my life could be up for a big change. When my time came, I was received by a very calm and poised Prime Minister in the meeting room adjacent to his office. We both sat on the sofas and he allowed me to present the rationale for my idea. I explained that I had the conviction that the time was right to re-engage with investors as the signs coming from the economy were clearly indicating the program's success. The negative flows that had contributed to the very high levels of government and external debt were turning around. And I explained why I thought I had the right skill set to do the job. It was not very difficult to get the Prime Minister to agree. He concurred that it made sense but had to run the idea through the Minister of Finance. We parted with a very cordial handshake.

A few weeks later, back in London in the trading floor of the investment bank where I was working, I received a call from the Portuguese Ambassador inviting me for a dinner with the Minister of Finance in the Portuguese Embassy. I had a strong suspicion about what he wanted to discuss with me. After a lively dinner with the Minister's staff, the Ambassador and a famous economist who had been the Minister's colleague, The Minister asked me to wait for him in a room and invited me to take up the job. This was done in a very no nonsense kind of way. He explained what would be expected of me in a very straight and to the point manner that I really appreciated. I was very excited and felt privileged to be part of this team. I had a very high degree of conviction that the task ahead was going to be successful and that my life would gain, finally after all these years following the PhD, a higher meaning.

References

1. Jeromin Zettelmeyer. "The Greek Debt Restructuring: An Autopsy." *Working Paper Peterson Institute for International Economics* 13–8 (August 2013).
2. Jorge Correia da Cunha and Claudia Braz. "The Evolution of Public Expenditure: Portugal in the Euro Area Context." *Bank of Portugal Economic Bulletin* (winter 2012).

3. Ricardo Reis. "The Portuguese Slump and Crash and the Euro Crisis." *NBER Working Paper* 19288 (August 2013).
4. Martin Eichenbaum, Sergio Rebelo and Carlos de Resende. "The Portuguese Crisis and the IMF", *Independent Evaluation Office of the International Monetary Fund* (July 2016).
5. Deutsche Bundesbank. "The dynamics of the Bundesbank's Target 2 balance." *Deutsche Bundesbank Monthly Report* (March 2011).
6. Deutsche Bundesbank. "Target2 balances in the Eurosystem." *Deutsche Bundesbank Annual Report* (2011).
7. European Central Bank. *"Annual Report"* (2011).
8. www.pordata.pt
9. Klaus Schwab ed. *The Global Competitiveness Report 2016–2017*. World Economic Forum, 2016.
10. International Monetary Fund. "Portugal: First Review Under the Extended Arrangement." *IMF Country Report* 11/279 (September 2011).
11. Directorate-General for Economic and Financial Affairs, European Commission. "The Economic Adjustment Programme for Portugal." *Occasional Papers 79* (June 2011).
12. International Monetary Fund. "Portugal: Letter of Intent, Memorandum of Economic and Financial Policies, and Technical Memorandum of Understanding." (17 May 2011).
13. Roberto A. De Santis. "A Measure of Redenomination Risk." *European Central Bank Working Paper* 1785 (April 2015).
14. Moody's investors services. "Rating Action: Moody's downgrades Portugal to Ba2 with a negative outlook from Baa1." July 5, 2011. https://www.moodys.com/research/Moodys-downgrades-Portugal-to-Ba2-with-a-negative-outlook-from?docid=PR_222043
15. Matthias Sobolewski and Dina Kiryakidou. "S&P downgrades nine euro zone countries." Reuters Business News, April 14, 2012.
16. Moody's investors services. "Moody's adjusts ratings of 9 European sovereigns to capture downside risks." February 13, 2012. https://www.moodys.com/research/Moodys-adjusts-ratings-of-9-European-sovereigns-to-capture-downside%2D%2Dpr_237716

CHAPTER 2

Warming Up

Abstract In this chapter, I explain the economic and social situation in Portugal at the beginning of 2012. The situation is dramatic, characterized by very high levels of unemployment, especially among the youth. I describe the Portuguese Debt Management Office that I am about to lead: the Treasury and Debt Management Office for Portugal ("IGCP"). In London, before joining the IGCP, I started preparing for the job. I had very useful preparatory meetings with professionals that had followed closely the emerging markets crisis of the 1990s. Our first challenge was to decide how to present the Portuguese situation to investors in view of re-establishing credibility in the markets. Our second challenge would be to rebuild a diversified investor base. We had to look for new investors to replace the investors that used to buy Portuguese government bonds before the crisis and were burnt by price moves, rating downgrades and orders to sell coming from their bosses and shareholders. In the meantime, the European government bond market situation started to contaminate Spain and Italy, triggering Draghi's "whatever it takes" speech. The fact that our Troika funding would only last up to September 2013 triggered our first transaction: a bond exchange.

Keywords PIGS • ECB • Draghi • Whatever it takes • Bond exchange • Rating agencies

J. M. Rato, *The European Debt Crisis*,
https://doi.org/10.1007/978-3-030-61174-3_2

At the beginning of 2012, the Portuguese economy was adjusting quickly, mostly in what concerned external accounts. As a consequence, the economic contraction was higher than what was expected when the program was designed.[1] Notably, unemployment was peaking at a higher rate than anticipated. The unemployment rate that was projected to stay at close to 13% was now approaching 16%. More than half the unemployed were without a job for more than a year, which represented a very sharp increase relative to 2011. A substantial amount of people were on the verge of losing their unemployment benefits, leaving them in a more desperate situation. Employment had been contracting at close to 2% year on year in 2011 and was now contracting at a rate close to 4%.[2] The rate of employment destruction had just accelerated at the start of 2012, with close to 300,000 jobs lost between 2011 and 2012. Temporary contracts were not being renewed, bringing lots of Portuguese workers and their families into situations of extreme financial stress. This situation affected the young people disproportionately and brought some to look into emigration as the sole solution to their economic woes. Youth unemployment was already high, increasing from 16.7%, for the under-25s, to 30.2% in 2011, and in 2012 it reached a peak of 37.9%. The destruction of jobs was affecting mostly the workers that did not have a university degree. But still, in 2012 the rate of unemployment among workers with an undergraduate degree was 11.6%. Emigration had been increasing. During the course of 2011, 100,970 people emigrated and in 2012 the numbers climbed to 121,418 (they would peak in 2014 at 1 34,624). The lowest point for real wages was in 2012.[3]

This was the bleak picture for my country at the time I had decided to return after 17 years outside. As you might expect, the mood was very negative. There was a lot of tension in the air. To add to the woes, as the budget expenditures looked difficult to control in 2011, compromising the achievement of the Troika targets, the government included in the 2012 budget additional pension and public sector cuts. In Portugal wages are paid in 14 installments (the usual 12 months plus summer holiday and Christmas subsidies). For 2012, the government included in the budget a

[1] For a more extensive comparison between program projections and outcomes see "Portugal, ex-post evaluation of exceptional access under the 2011 extended arrangement – press release; staff report; and authorities views", IMF, September 2016.

[2] Annual Board Report from the Bank of Portugal (2012).

[3] Data available in Pordata using the National Statistics Institute data.

two-year suspension of these two extra wage payments. This measure was equivalent to a 12% average cut.[4] It would only fully affect public sector workers and pensioners earning more than €1100 per month for social equity reasons. To understand the social impact of these cuts, you have to consider that in 2012 there were close to a million pensioners in Portugal and 700,000 civil servants out of a population of 10.5 million. So, close to 35% of the population had the potential to be affected by the policies. And even the ones with less income, not affected directly, lived in the fear that they could be hit next. These cuts followed similar measures in 2010 that had reduced public sector wages between 3.5% and 10% depending on earnings. In addition, overtime compensation was reduced and bonus and wage premiums were eliminated.

These cuts had a deep impact on public opinion and in the Treasury and Debt Management Office for Portugal ("IGCP"). Some of the workers at the agency had accumulated cuts in their earnings in the previous two years of more than 22%. The morale had every reason to be quite low. Nevertheless, I have to say that in a good number of my colleagues, including the ones more linked to debt management, there was always a lot of enthusiasm with the task at hand: regaining market access to the medium and long term government bond market. They were relieved to be lead by a new board they could count on and with a more positive attitude. The previous leadership looked depressed at times according to some of the employee accounts. Even so, I found at the IGCP a positive vibe from the start.

The IGCP as an institution had a very good domestic and international reputation and did not lack in technical credibility. It had been founded in 1996 by a good friend of mine, Vítor Bento. Sixteen years later, Vítor still exerted a strong influence on the agency. It was evident that I could not join the IGCP without speaking to him and listening carefully to all his tips. In addition, one of the IGCP founders remained in the board and was going to be my colleague. The IGCP had been created as an autonomous agency reporting to the Ministry of Finance. The intention was to give it some technical autonomy and the capacity to hire the right human resources in competition with the banking sector. To attract the best specialists in fixed income risk analysis, capital markets and trading, the agency had to be granted autonomy from the Ministry of Finance, allowing for a

[4] As estimated by the Troika. See the second review under the extended agreement from December 2011.

higher management flexibility. The IGCP had been created with the objective of preparing the Portuguese government for issuing bonds in euros.[5] The founders had travelled across Europe looking for the best in class debt management offices for inspiration. The autonomy and technical independence were very important components of its ethos and made its employees proud. This autonomy was even more important for them now, following a period where they felt there had been excessive political interference. The IGCP was respected by its peers worldwide for its technical skills and knowledge. When the IMF and the World Bank decided to look for case studies for their debt management guidelines, the IGCP was included.[6] It was one of the first debt management offices to develop more advanced risk management tools like the risk benchmark.

Following my conversation with the Minister of Finance at the Portuguese Embassy in London, I had been looking very closely at the new law that was being drafted for the IGCP. The motivation for the change was that the institutional framework that had been chosen to ensure the autonomy of my future home was no longer suitable in light of changes introduced by the Troika. A new institutional wrap would have to be selected for the administrative and financial autonomy to be preserved. For me this was an important pre-condition to be able to perform our mission and to maintain the focus and morale of the employees.

This new law would include more responsibilities in the IGCP's scope of work. It would add tasks linked with controlling and monitoring the state-owned enterprises ("SOEs") leverage and the management of their derivative (swaps) portfolios. This new role was introduced by the Troika program. The intention was to deal with the hairy legacy problems that existed in the public sector companies, especially in what concerned their portfolio of derivatives, and to prevent the exaggerated use of derivatives and debt by SOEs in the future. When we came into office, the portfolio of derivatives of the SOEs showed negative valuation of €3 Billion (a bit less than 2% of Portugal's GDP of the time). This was the amount that these companies would have to pay the banks, that acted as their counterparties in these swap transactions, in case they wanted to close them. If they kept them alive, they would keep running the risk that the situation

[5] The IGCP in 2012 included not only the Debt Management Office but also the government's treasury function that had been added later on.

[6] See Guidelines for Public Debt Management: Accompanying Document, IMF (2012).

could get worse for the taxpayers. I mention the taxpayers since these companies were mostly experiencing annual losses and would need outside money to close these transactions and pay the banks.

In addition, many of these SOEs had accumulated high levels of debt. To increase the seriousness of the situation, an important part of the SOEs' debt had rating triggers and other early redemption triggers. When these triggers were actioned investors could demand to be immediately repaid. Triggers had been actioned when the State was downgraded, in 2012. Portugal, at the time, did not have the funds to repay most of its SOE debt in advance. At the insistence of international investors that wanted to get their cash back upfront, the domestic banks had to replace them, taking over their positions. The transfer of these exposures to domestic banks had a negative impact on the credit available to the economy, deepening the recession. When we joined the IGCP, there were still some international banks threatening to activate other, more arguable, triggers.

The board of the IGCP, which I was invited to lead, was consistent of two other members: Cristina Casalinho and António Pontes Correia. Cristina was, at the time, a very respected economist working for a domestic bank. She had the reputation of being very straightforward, honest and able to quote all the relevant figures off the top of her head. I could vouch this was true, as in my previous investment banking job, when I wanted to bring an international investor to speak about the Portuguese economy, Cristina had always been my choice. Her appointment was an idea of the State Secretary for Finance, Maria Luis Albuquerque, but I immediately agreed to bring her on board. I thought that for the job ahead a solid credible economist would be essential. And, on a personal level, the people we knew in common all assured me she was a good and reliable person. Our other colleague in the board, António, had been one of the original founders of the IGCP in 1996. He had always been a top civil servant at the Ministry of Finance and knew well how to operate within the civil service in general and the Ministry of Finance in particular. He was very respected by the employees and perceived as a carrier of the IGCP ethos and a great defender of the agency within the Ministry of Finance. He had the reputation of having very strong ethics. Again, all friends we had in common only had very good things to say about him and assured me I could trust him with closed eyes. In reality, during the years I stayed at the IGCP, the board always acted as one and always looked for consensus and unity. We took seriously the saying that three sticks together are more difficult to break. I am still a very good friend of both of them and the story that I tell in this book is in large part a common story, considering, of course, that any imprecisions and mistakes in telling it are my own.

I was still in London, in the apartment I had been living in for the last four years, when I received a call from a very special old friend. It was António Borges. António was a very respected economist, a Stanford PhD, brilliant and a very good speaker. He had been the dean of INSEAD in the 1980s and 1990s. He had joined Goldman Sachs in 2000 as a partner in London. It was at Goldman Sachs that I had met him and first interacted with him. He had lately been the head of the European department at the IMF during the time when Dominique Strauss Kahn had been the Managing Director. I had kept in touch with him since our times at Goldman Sachs. António was now an advisor to the government and was working very closely with the Minister of Finance. I witnessed later on that he had a strong influence in the government. He called me to insist that I should start as soon as possible. Actually, more than that, he wanted to ask me what the hell I was waiting for to join the effort. The economy was recovering quickly from its chronic external disequilibrium and as it attained a balance, or even an external surplus, everything would fall into place. It was urgent to start speaking to investors, who he believed were ready to start doing their homework on the country, to analyze what was happening in Portugal, and that we should kick-start the process of re-establishing market access for our bonds. I explained that, on my side, I was ready to start but that I was waiting to be officially appointed. I conveyed to him that I was aware of the urgency and was not being complacent. I believe he was reassured and understood that he had to apply his pressure over another node in the decision tree.

In London, I was preparing to face the challenges awaiting us in the next few years. The first challenge we were facing was how to tell the story of what had happened in Portugal—how to explain the causes that brought the country to the situation it was in and what policies were being implemented to solve it. We had to convince professional investors that the path the country had taken would be followed with conviction and that the situation could be reversed.

The second challenge was to rebuild the Portuguese investors' base. As we have seen in the previous chapter, Portugal had gone through a series of rating downgrades, culminating in February 2012 with Moody's last downgrade. The process coincided with discussions regarding the possibility of a disorderly default in Greece. Most of the investors that had historically engaged with Portugal were forced to sell bonds, or at least were under pressure to do so. That was the reason why the price of the bonds became so depressed. The boards of European banks and insurance companies, under pressure from the shareholders, were pressuring their treasuries and investment departments to decrease the exposure to the European periphery, including Portugal. The pressure was so high and the market so thin, with so few buyers, that some of the insurance companies would take months to decrease their exposure, selling the bonds each time an opportunity arose. Obviously, these investors would take some time to reinvest and would not be the first ones knocking at Portugal's door when it would restart the issuance of bonds. The challenge was to find some new investors that had not been holders of the bonds on the way down and were not "traumatized" by the periods during which the bond prices suffered.

With those challenges in mind, and with some time in London before relocating fully to Lisbon, I started to prepare myself to get to a point where I could, with my team, present to the Minister of Finance a plan for regaining access to the bond markets. I had the conviction that I should try to speak to people that had been involved in similar processes in the past, for instance in Latin America following the 1990s Tequila crisis. I was following the old and tested advice of not trying to reinvent the wheel.

I was lucky to have a few friends that could help. One of these friends had another friend who was a portfolio manager at an emerging markets fund. He was located in London and could easily arrange for some time to discuss with me over breakfast. I explained what I was looking for, we had a nice chat and a few days later he contacted me again. He told me that his boss, the fund's owner, an old timer from Salomon Brothers that had followed closely some of the Latin American case studies in the 1990s, was happy to have breakfast with us and discuss.

We met in a very nice and modern breakfast place in a hotel in Marylebone, the kind of place that had been opening in quantity during the last decade in London. Immediately, as we sat down, he asked me what would be my pitch for Portugal. How would I sell the story to an investor? I was taken a bit by surprise by the immediacy of the question. But I knew I could not hesitate and dived into my first pitch. I explained how Portugal got to the situation it was in and explained what the government was doing to deal with the excess leverage, that the flows were starting to revert and the one that was adjusting faster was the external deficit. I explained why this adjustment path would prove resilient and that the

Portuguese population believed in Europe and would ultimately prefer to keep the country within the euro. He listened attentively and then said one important thing that stayed in my mind thereafter: "it is all very nice but your speech lacks something that investors will need to understand before investing in Portuguese bonds. Eventually they will have to be comfortable that growth will come after the severe contraction. And they will need to have an idea where this growth will be coming from. Your pitch lacks this; it lacks hope in the future." This comment was crucial for the way we tried to look at the Portuguese situation and how we would describe it to investors later on. Investors would not invest in a country that was only doing the homework but would not be able to grow out of its debt. To commit to medium and long term bonds, they needed to believe that in the context of the low inflation environment in the Eurozone, Portugal would be able to grow out of its debt situation. To build this belief they needed to identify what would be the source of this growth. This would be essential. And I believe it proved decisive later on when we had constant and regular contacts with investors. As we parted, he promised that he would introduce me to other people that would be useful to me during my preparation period.

And he did. The first one was a very well-known lawyer that had been linked with a few high-profile restructuring situations. When he contacted me, I graciously thanked him but explained that it was not the right moment to speak to him. I was not expecting Portugal to need his services and the simple fact of speaking to him could bring negative perception risks. He understood and said that if I ever needed him I would know where I could find him.

The second contact was very useful. He was a high-level executive in an investment bank and had been, again, involved in assisting some Latin American countries in the 1990s following the Tequila crisis. He received me in his office and was most useful in giving me his view of the situation in Europe. It was not very containing though. He mentioned that one of his missions in the bank had been to come to Europe and check what the plan was to deal with the crisis in the periphery. He mentioned: "I traveled all over, to Brussels, to Frankfurt, to Paris. But after a few months, I understood: there was no plan!" This gave me an important insight into the context in which I would be working in the next few years. And from then on, it kept me on the alert. In general, I became skeptical on the existence of a plan coming from Brussels, Berlin, Paris or any decision-making centers in Europe. This helped me to be always prepared for a worst-case scenario where we would mostly depend on ourselves and would not expect a white knight to come to our rescue—even if that white knight eventually would come up, in some situations, like when Mario Draghi made his "whatever it takes" speech or when our European partners agreed to extend the maturities of the official debt that Portugal had borrowed from other European Union and Eurozone countries.

The third challenge had much less visibility. As I have mentioned, we had to deal with legacy issues from the SOEs and the autonomous region of Madeira. The latter was almost mechanical as the Ministry of Finance had designed a funded plan for Madeira. The money was to be used for specific means in, for example, the health sector. The transfers were done against invoices and the IGCP had to control the process. Two areas where the IGCP had some scope for action were the derivatives portfolio and some loans from external banks which had prepayment triggers that were debatable (according to them, not according to us). The lenders were looking for contractual clauses in the debt documents that could allow them to be repaid in full immediately. All these issues had to be understood in the context of an adjustment program where cash was scarce. Prepaying any bonds was something to avoid. The plan was to respect all commitments but never to prepay when the State did not have to do so, avoiding cash to go out of our accounts.

Regarding the derivatives portfolio, we prepared ourselves by looking to hire professionals with specific skills. We needed someone that could eventually, working with external consultants, build internal pricing capabilities. These capabilities would be crucial in any future negotiation process. Even before we started our jobs, the board got together and identified a candidate. We identified a very technical professional that had stayed in a bank that had been intervened by the State. He proved a very valuable hire. In addition, we hired a markets person that had left Citi as it reduced its presence in Portugal. She was to act as a project manager, both in the derivatives negotiations and looking through all the remaining SOE prepayment risks. In addition, a new head of legal joined the team. The previous head of legal had been poached by the IMF team in Portugal as an advisor. When we looked for a replacement we were looking for someone with capital markets experience so she could also help with the derivatives situations. Again, she was a great hire that has helped the IGCP to become more and more agile in the debt markets.

The previous head of legal was not staying far, as the IMF had set up his Lisbon headquarters in our building. This fact brought a few demonstrations to our doors. We had to leave the building undercover through the crowds a few times. But we have to say that normally the crowds were outnumbered by the police officers.

During our first weeks as a newly elected board, we were called to the Ministry of Finance. We had a meeting with the State Secretary for the Treasury and with some officers representing a European bad bank (servicing problematic legacy assets). They had all sorts of arguments to try to justify a request for their loans to an SOE to be repaid immediately. Their team looked like a typical distressed debt team, overexcited by strong personal incentives linked to their performance on the assets' recovery value. As the meeting progressed, their insistence turned more and more aggressive, verging on becoming rude and almost insulting. They were treating the Portuguese State as a misbehaved borrower and were starting to use their bullying techniques against our team. We had to remind them that they were in the presence of State officials. We threatened to end the meeting swiftly and they calmed down. After that brief trip to the dark side, we decided with the State Secretary that from then on all these types of meetings were to be held at the IGCP, never again in the Ministry, and only in our presence, to protect the deserved dignity of elected government officials.

The fourth challenge we were facing was more immediate. The adjustment program designed by the Troika covered the State's financing needs up to September 2013, exactly when a bond had to be repaid. The amount of the bond redemption was substantial and was only partially covered by the cash to be received from the Troika. Any country under an IMF program has to always show how it intends to finance its needs for the following year. So, our most immediate challenge was to present a plan on how we were intending to get the cash needed to repay this bond. And we had to present it by September 2012.

In the meantime, the Portuguese ten-year bond that was offering investors a yield higher than 13% in March reached briefly below 10% in June. The maximum had been 17% in January, but this was a reflection of the forced selling of bonds that we discussed previously, and 13% had been a more consistent yield offered to investors acquiring bonds in the market. So, investors seemed to be giving some credit to the fact that the massive twin deficits of the past were starting to revert. The price volatility was still very high, as the press headlines would keep bringing the bonds back to 13%. But spikes in yields happened more and more episodically. The trend had been positive for Portugal in the first half of 2012 in terms of market stabilization and the same was valid for Ireland. In the case of Greece, the bonds continued at levels that showed they were untouchable by investors. It was clear they were not benefitting from the same dynamics as Portugal and Ireland. Some investors started to believe there was an opportunity at these very distressed prices for Portuguese government bonds and were looking to get involved. Probably these investors were some of the more knowledgeable and analytical hedge funds that had the tools to evaluate the country's economic performance at the beginning of the adjustment program. Ireland was at a more advanced stage. Some market specialists were telling us to follow their example and to try to get our story as closely associated with theirs as possible. The problem was that during the first semester of 2012 Italy and Spain were starting to show some signs of market stress. Investors were demanding more and more yield to invest in their bonds. This was a big issue as neither country was within a Troika program. They had to rely fully on the market for their financing needs, which was not the case either for Portugal or for Ireland. Both Spain and Italy were by June 2012 getting dangerously close (or over in the case of Italy) to 6%. At these yields their cost of funding would start to be perceived as a threat to debt sustainability. In their cases, given the sizes of their annual financing needs, it was not obvious that Europe would have the capacity to give them the right amount of support. That was scary. And what would be the aftershocks on the European banking sector of such big countries needing assistance? Given that banks in Europe had sizeable exposures to those sovereigns, would they drag European banks into a systemic crisis? The impact on the banks could then revert on the sovereigns, which would have to support the banks. And so on, and so on. Just remember what had happened to Portuguese bond prices when rating actions caused forced selling by banks and insurance companies. In June 2012, as Portuguese and Irish bonds were starting to be picked up by some buyers, there was no good news from Greece, and Italy and Spain became the focus of market talk. These two countries were the ones that would have a wider impact if their bonds fell into a situation of stress.

Our board had been announced in April 2012 but we were only officially nominated in June. As expected, we were immediately requested to present a plan for regaining market access. It was clear to us when writing down our plan that we had two constraints. The first was, as already mentioned, that it would be difficult in the short term to attract back European investors to Portuguese debt. Later on in the process, we organized a roadshow in Frankfurt, which included a breakfast with investors and the

State Secretary, that was quite empty. When inquiring why there were so few investors, one participant candidly replied, "because investing in Portugal at this stage means taking unemployment risk." What he meant was that after what had happened only a few months before to the Portuguese bond market, experiencing an extended period of panic selling, anyone that invested would risk being fired in case the bonds lost value again. You had to be brave, and/or very convinced, to be the first one to take that step out of the group of big European institutional investors, including insurance companies, asset managers or banks.

The second constraint was that Portuguese investors did not seem to have much capacity at that moment in time to make a difference. Only domestic banks could move the needle in terms of buying volumes and most of them were limited in their capacity. So, we had to prepare a plan targeting new investors either externally or domestically. That is why our plan was pointing toward US investors and emerging markets funds. Again, we were looking at precedents in the Irish and Icelandic bond market where we had seen US investors playing a role in recent bond issuances. In what concerned the domestic market, we were looking to re-activate the retail market through the issuance of certificates. These were retail market instruments sold to moms and pops, involving low average investment volumes per investor, which had historically been an instrument for the middle class to channel its savings. The interest payments of these certificates had been reduced in the past unilaterally when the domestic banks became worried about deposit flight. Part of our proposal was to re-engage with this customer base and restore attractive interest rates for buyers of the certificates.

In parallel, we started working on the roadshow presentation so that we could start our contacts with investors. We were lucky to have in our team Cristina and her long experience heading the economic research team of one of the domestic banks. The way we were looking to address investors was a crucial part of our strategy: it had to be candid and factual. In that sense, we wanted it to be very different from the propaganda tone of previous presentations by the Portuguese Debt Management Office. A previous presentation included an entire slide about how Portugal was manufacturing parts for the space shuttle. In our opinion, it was borderline. We wanted to keep our new presentation closer to earth!

The first chapter of the presentation we would call later the "mea culpa". It was all about the starting point for the adjustment program and how Portugal got to its current condition: the accumulation of external deficits and private sector debt, government deficits, low productivity growth. We explained how low productivity growth was linked to an imbalanced allocation of resources to low productivity non-tradable sectors. All this was illustrated by graphs reflecting actual data. Then we explained how the economic and financial assistance program was designed to deal with these macroeconomic imbalances. And why the program was implementable in the Portuguese social and political context. Then, we would approach how the economic structure was changing as exports grew since 2010 and how this growth in exports was partially compensating for the fall in domestic demand. This was the source of "hope" that was missing in my discussions with the fund owner in London. We explained that the economy was correcting the imbalances outlined in the "mea culpa" section and that jobs were being destroyed in the labor-intensive non-tradable sectors. These were the low-productivity sectors that had seen excess investment in the period before the crisis. All these would remind the economists, working for the investors, of similar adjustments in the past. We hoped they would spot the similarities with successful adjustment sequences in other countries. Then, we dug into more detail, to describe the external adjustment that was being strengthened by the export sector performance. We outlined that the external adjustment was stronger and faster than initially projected and that the goods and services account was moving toward a balance in Portugal for the first time since the Second World War. In addition, this export performance was based on sectoral diversification. The Portuguese export sector was diversified and modern, which came as a surprise to a lot of investors, as even one widely read current affairs magazine was, at the time, still speaking about Portuguese exports being concentrated in the traditional, labor-intensive, sectors, like textiles. We showed that Portugal had been successful in diversifying exports. Electronics and mechanical machinery were 15% of exports, vehicle and parts were 12%, textiles were 9% and footwear were 4%. In addition, even geographically Portugal was diversifying its export destinations, exporting a higher share to countries outside of Europe.

Then we explained how structural reforms would sustain competitiveness gains. These reforms would make Portugal more attractive for foreign direct investment in the future and continue to boost exports. We concluded our presentation by looking into how fiscal discipline would eventually bring down the debt over GDP. We would end by describing the

State's financing needs for the next few years and how we were expecting to fund those.

As we were preparing ourselves for the challenges ahead, Draghi made his historical speech in London on 26 July: "within our mandate, the ECB [European Central Bank] is ready to do whatever it takes to preserve the euro. And believe me, it will be enough."[7]As we had seen, the bond market vigilantes had been on Italy's case, mostly, but also on Spain's case in the last few months. And given the size of these two countries and their share of the Eurozone economy, they were perceived to have the potential to put the euro itself at risk. To preserve the single currency was the motivation behind this speech. And, in addition, to provide some consistency to the promise, a week after the speech the ECB announced a new program called Outright Monetary Transactions ("OMT"), which consisted in the purchase bonds of member countries if needed. The OMT would be described as the ECB willingness to use the "bazooka," meaning that if an investor would be looking to bet against the bonds of the Eurozone countries, like Soros did against the sterling in the 1990s, and implicitly bet against the euro survival, the ECB would be willing to use all its balance sheet capacity against these speculative forces. If you are a fund betting against the prices of Italian bonds and you know that on the other side there is a central bank that is willing to buy unlimited amounts of these bonds to counter you, you will think twice. Looking to benefit from lower prices in those circumstances can prove quite unfruitful. As the ECB threatened to use its full force, the ten-year Italian bonds that were being sold with an annual yield of close to 7% quickly came back to 5%. Even if the speech was a game changer in terms of systemic risk, it would not be enough to bring the weaker countries back into the market but would prevent them from being dragged by a bigger systemic wave engulfing the euro area.

The first Troika review in which we participated was the fifth review. The reviews, where we would have to interact with the IMF, the European Commission and the ECB, took place on a quarterly basis. The IGCP was called during every review for two main meetings: the first one, close to the beginning of the review, where the expected cash outflows and inflows for the near future were discussed. After looking at all outflows and cash inflows from the State, the financing needs were calculated. Then, we

[7]Verbatim of the remarks made by Draghi from Speech at the Global Investment Conference in London, 26 July 2012, as in the site of the ECB.

would check how much of the Troika cash was expected to be used. This cash was coming in, as we have seen previously, in a staggered manner. The second meeting in which the IGCP participated would close the review, as it calculated the expected future debt dynamics. It summarized all the mission discussions concerning State deficits, cash needed for SOEs or other expenses outside the central government expenditure scope (not included in the deficit), and projected the economic parameters (GDP growth, average interest rate on the debt), to produce an expected debt dynamics path.

The first of these meetings was particularly important during the fifth review. It was the first review in which, after looking into all cash inflows and outflows for the next year, a gap would be detected. There was not enough cash coming from the Troika to cover the September 2013 bond redemption. The IGCP was then called to plan for an alternative source of funds with the objective of covering this gap. It was our first participation and we were playing quite a central role.

To prepare for this meeting our first instinct was to speak with our colleagues in Greece and Ireland that had already gone through a similar exercise. When we called them, they were both very useful. This was the first of more regular contacts that we would maintain with our counterparts in these countries during our tenure. They explained to us the different sensitivities within the Troika to the alternative instruments available to finance the September 2013 gap. For instance, as we would experience later in the meeting, the ECB was quite averse to the increase in the stock of Treasury Bills. These would end up in the local banks and eventually as collateral for the ECB lending to the banks as we discussed in the previous chapter. The Greeks alerted us to how sensitive the ECB would be to this topic.

In reality, we worked along two different alternatives. The first one, which was the obvious route, involved the presentation of a compromise package that would include a moderate increase in the Treasury Bills stock, the issuance of a Medium Term Note, a bond, for domestic insurance and pension funds and the re-activation of the domestic retail market. Alternatively, we discussed with the technical issuance team at the IGCP if we could offer a proposal to extend the maturity of the September 2013 bond. This latter proposal was a bit like the Columbus egg. If the cash deficit we would face in 2013 was due to the bond repayment, what if we could convince a high enough proportion of investors in the bond to extend the maturity into the future? To give some consistency to this possibility, we looked into where the bonds had been placed at issuance. It had originally been a 15-year maturity bond that had been issued in a relatively concentrated manner to mostly domestic investors. This could facilitate things as domestic investors might have incentives to keep the position and continue to benefit from the positive carry (high interest).

So, when we came to the Troika meeting, we presented two alternative plans. Plan A, a plan that should not have been far from their expectations, even if there was a clear willingness to push for the issuance of international bonds, possibility that was still recognized as remote. And plan B, which was more original and we expected would gather the audience preferences. The issue with plan B was that we could not guarantee it would work as it depended on the voluntary participation of investors. We could try to sound the market but there would always be a certain degree of uncertainty regarding its execution.

As expected, plan A was received with no enthusiasm and plan B was acclaimed. But we were careful to put all the stress on plan A and reduce expectations around plan B for the reasons mentioned. The next day we had an invitation for breakfast from the head of the IMF mission. They really liked our plan B and were curious to understand why we were so non-committal. I mentioned that this was not a plan but just an idea that we did not know if it would work in practice. But we guaranteed that we would put all our energy in trying to make it work. I had the sensation that the IMF team was more relieved.

From that moment on, we worked tirelessly in trying to understand what type of market support we could have for the transaction. We looked carefully into the list of initial investors in the bond and tried to assess if a high share of the bonds was still in the same hands. Then we sounded the market. With enough confidence, we announced a transaction on 3 October 2012, our first big transaction. It was an offer to exchange bonds that would redeem on 23 September 2013, for existing bonds that would only have to redeem on 10 October 2015. The transaction was a big success, pushing forward €3.76 billion in bond repayments. Moreover, 39% of the total was exchanged, which showed a high investor participation. We were now comfortably covered for cash for the next year. We could approach the market with no sense of urgency. In addition, we started building our credibility with the Troika by executing the much desired plan B. Our first big challenge had been overcome. In our presentation we titled the transaction: "Successful exchange offer: paving the way for Portugal to access long-term debt market."

References

1. International Monetary Fund. "Portugal, Third Review" (March 2012).
2. www.pordata.pt
3. www.ine.pt
4. Banco de Portugal. "Annual Report, The Portuguese Economy, 2012." (2013).
5. International Monetary Fund. "Portugal: Ex Post Evaluation of Exceptional Access Under the 2011 Extended Arrangement – Press Release; Staff Report; and Authorities Views." *IMF Country Report* no 16/302 (September 2016).
6. International Monetary Fund and The World Bank. "Guidelines for Public Debt Management: Accompanying Document" (November 2002).
7. International Monetary Fund. "Portugal, Fifth Review." (March 2012).
8. Sonal Badhan. "Portugal Outlook: Ghost of Debt-Restructuring Lingers." *Global Economic Outlook,* Roubini Global Economics, December 18, 2012.

CHAPTER 3

Investors

Abstract This chapter focuses on describing the interactions with the investor community during the process of rebuilding trust in Portugal. In the fall of 2012, we were ready to start meeting with investors and organize roadshows. It was to be the start of a medium to long term process aimed at restoring credibility with the investor community. To do so we chose a transparent, candid and fact-based approach. Given our massive financing needs for the next few years we were looking for repeated support from investors, so building trust was essential. I describe our first roadshows and meetings with investors that influenced deeply our style when interacting with investors: London, Tokyo and New York. The topics discussed with investors would change with circumstances in Portugal and in different investor geographies. The fall of 2012 saw massive protests in Portugal and social cohesion became an important issue for investors. I explain how different types of investors play different roles at different stages of the market normalization process.

Keywords Bond investors • Bond roadshows • Investor community • Investor diversification • Bond marketing • Sovereign credit

Following the preparation of a plan to regain market access, the drafting of an investor presentation, and given that we already had some results of the adjustment program to discuss with investors, we were ready to start

J. M. Rato, *The European Debt Crisis*,
https://doi.org/10.1007/978-3-030-61174-3_3

hitting the road and schedule some meetings. Our first meetings occurred during the summer and consisted of isolated investors that would come to visit us at the Treasury and Debt Management Office ("IGCP") office. They would normally include us as part of a visit that brought them to the State Secretary for Finance, to the State Secretary to the Prime Minister that had responsibility for the interactions with the Troika, to the IMF officer in Lisbon and to the Bank of Portugal. Later on, the visits became more sophisticated; investors would schedule meetings with the head of the foreign investment agency, the opposition party representatives, parliamentarians, ex-ministers and even opinion makers that voiced their opposition to the program in the media.

We were aware that we were just starting a process of multiple interactions with investors. We knew that to achieve success in our effort to rebuild market access, our relationship with investors could not be touch and go, but would have to be a medium to long term relationship based on repeated interactions through time. More than anything, we would need to rebuild credibility with the investor community. They would have to trust us. Only if we managed to build a capital of confidence would we be able to place the big amounts of debt we needed to place to become self-reliable again. One transaction, one issuance of debt, would clearly not be enough; we had to issue debt repeatedly in the future. To manage to do so, we aimed to rebuild an investor base that would support us through time. To achieve that, we would have to be trusted.

At the start of the process, I was invited by the CFO of a Portuguese bank for lunch. He offered to make a big effort to help the Portuguese State—he would support our first issuance in the market with an important amount, according to him. I swiftly inquired about the volume he would be willing to make available to us. He mentioned proudly: "something in the area of 200 million," and checked my reaction. I thanked him but told him that the State needed billions and that hundreds of millions would make no difference. His big effort would not change our life in the slightest so it was probably not worthwhile.

As professionals, the entire team at the IGCP believed in the importance of being transparent with investors. We joined the Portuguese Debt Management Office at a time when the Portuguese State reputation had just reached the bottom and the authorities were working hard to rebuild it. Experienced investors in sovereign bonds know the importance of meeting the State officials in a country that is just coming out of distress. They understand the value of meeting the people, the faces, behind a country's effort to recover from the bottom. They want to see if State officials understand the reasons why the country is in that specific position and what needs to be done to come out of it. They are keen to understand if the people with responsibility in the country have the right technical skills for the job ahead, if they are committed to go through the tribulations that will come with the tasks they have to complete and if they are honest and trustworthy. Investors that are looking to invest in the debt of countries coming out of trouble have seen hundreds of officials in different countries at different times. They have been lied to a few times and have met people that were unprepared or weak in their convictions. They revisit their memories to identify the characteristics of successful cases, looking to confirm their investment convictions.

We knew how important it would be to be candid, technical, transparent. We knew it was crucial to be clear about the country's weaknesses and the risks to Portuguese government bond's performance, so that investors can build their case when taking the decision to invest. That was why our presentation was as much fact based as possible and that was why at the beginning we used to start our presentation with a section we called "mea culpa," which described realistically the negative starting point for the Portuguese economy at the beginning of the Troika program. We wanted to tell a story of pragmatism—Portugal was in trouble, why it was in trouble and what was being done to deal with it. We intended to regularly update investors about the process that the authorities were following to deal with the issues. And investors, when they were coming to Portugal, in their visits to the authorities, were looking to assess, face to face, the government's attitudes, knowledge, resilience and intentions. They know that the type of economic adjustment process Portugal was going through is quite tough politically and that the right degree of conviction on the part of the authorities is essential to reach results. They also know that these processes take time and that you need to maintain some pace of reforms and run the distance. They have seen some cases where recoveries from high debt were stopped in the middle and countries relapsed before getting to a safer place. That is why investor visits become more extensive as they become more engaged and start investing in bigger sizes.

I can remember a particular visit from a very relevant US investor. I scheduled a meeting with the Minister of Finance. We went there with Cristina and the State Secretary for Finance. During the meeting the

Minister of Finance and the investor got involved in a discussion about how far the adjustment process had gone and how far it still had to go. They plunged into technical economic indicators. The Minister showed in a graph the path that a particular indicator had taken. The investor followed with his eyes the shape of the two or three graphs that the Minister was showing him, his eyes jumping from paper to paper, from graph to graph. With a sweeping gesture of his hand, implying a "voila," the Minister concluded, something like "so you see, that is why I think there is still this time to go." The investor was in agreement; it all made sense to him. When we left the meeting room into the cold and vast Ministry corridor, the investor, still under the spell of the Minister's dialectic, told me that this was the most convincing Minister of Finance that he had ever met. Convincing in a technical sense of course. And this was not a small thing as the job of this professional, a chief investment officer in a major bond fund, was, in large scale, to travel around the world and meet different Ministers of Finance in different countries from Asia to Europe and Latin America. The investor was impressed and I believe he did not keep his perception to himself, contributing to the very good reputation our Minister was acquiring with investors.

On another note, and later in the process, we took a hedge fund manager with whom we had established a good relationship to a newly nominated official. She had been one of the earlier visitors to our offices during the summer of 2012 and we had visited her at the beginning of 2013 in her fund's offices. She was very knowledgeable and technical and always intellectually challenging. By the time we took her to visit the official, we had had several conversations and she had been following our work closely. We went into the meeting and the official was not very prepared and was a bit too candid, which can be a good thing but in this case he was discussing some inappropriate internal issues with an investor that did not really care. On the technical issues, he gave the impression that he had no deep knowledge or strategy. When we left the meeting, she turned to us and was reflective. When leaving the elevator and walking toward the door, she said, thinking aloud, something like "One bad official does not change much if the institutions are strong and he is surrounded by good ones. Do you agree?" We walked silently toward the street and said goodbye while she was getting into her taxi.

Besides the importance of technical trust, it is crucial for investors that the Debt Management Office, as their counterparty, keeps them posted on the risks. Investors do not like surprises. They can deal with uncertainty but keep a sour feeling if something happens that was not talked about as a possibility. They are compensated to take risks but like to have the risks properly identified beforehand. They prefer to avoid "unknown unknowns," quoting Donald Rumsfeld. These can have a huge impact on their trust of the issuer. If they suspect the issuer knew that some event was a possibility and never alerted them to it, they may prefer to reduce their exposure to the bonds. They try to avoid investments in a sovereign where there are too many of these unknowns and where they have trouble quantifying the risks they face. Do not forget that most professional investors do not act alone. There exists, usually, an investment governance. Investors have to take their investment proposals to an investment committee within their firm. They have to outline the investment risks to the committee members and the expected return on their investment, including what will happen in negative scenarios and in situations of market stress. Based on their assessment, the investment committee will reach a decision. If some scenario that was presented happens and the consequences are roughly in line with what was presented, too bad. But if some event takes place that was not outlined and has consequences for the return on the investment, the committee will inquire with the professional why this was not part of his presentation. He could be in trouble and it could make it difficult for him to go back later to the committee to propose increasing the investment size. Part of what you do at the Debt Management Office is to make it easier for investors to present your investment case to a committee.

In July 2013, as we will describe later on, the Minister of Finance resigned followed by the resignation of the Minister of Foreign Affairs, and the government was in a fragile position. When this happened, I received a call from an investor that worked for a Danish pension fund and had been a strong advocate of investing in Portugal. "Each time I have to invest in Bunds with such a low yield, my heart breaks." To keep returns for their pensioners, investors needed to look for higher yielding government bonds while still keeping an acceptable level of risk. They were very professional and thorough when conducting their due diligences on the Portuguese government bonds. She was on the phone and her first question was "Joao, why did you not warn me that this could happen?" It was not easy, probably one of the most difficult moments in my job as Head of the IGCP, to recognize that I had never expected this and so I had not outlined this risk. We always mentioned and explained the fragilities of a coalition government, but we had to accept we were not expecting this to happen in July 2013. We had just issued a bond in May and were flying in from a roadshow in the US. It was painful to have to acknowledge it, there on the phone, but it was the truth. From that point on, we started to pay more attention to the details of internal politics.

Our first roadshow, with scheduled investor meetings, was in London, and we were testing our presentation for the first time. I have to admit it was not a particularly good day. It allowed us to very quickly get into the right tune and professionalize our delivery. I still expressed some opinions that day, which is a big mistake. I understood that we had to be as objective as possible, and yes illustrate with experiences, sometimes even our own, but not to make it personal and never forget we were public officials. This would be the wrong way to establish relationships. It was a very important trip to prepare us for Tokyo and New York where we were heading next.

In Tokyo, we were at the IMF meetings and there were few investors present. An exception was a tea session in the lounge of the Tokyo Imperial Hotel. As expected in Tokyo, we had tea in style and the investor himself was very sophisticated in terms of economic knowledge, experience, manners and fashion sense. We were having tea and he spoke softly and in a very articulated manner. We spent most of the time looking at the debt redemption page of our presentation which included a time line ordering the years ahead and for each year a bar indicating how much Portugal would have to repay that year. The graph showed a very steep summit very close by in the future. It showed we did not have a lot of time to re-establish proper access to the market as we had to climb a very steep redemption wall: 2014 was challenging, 2015 more challenging and 2016 looked daunting. He told us that investors would prefer to wait and see if we could climb it instead of engaging with our bonds before 2016 and risk a Private Sector Involvement ("PSI") in case we could not survive the massive redemption commitments we were facing. He was telling me our job was pretty much impossible in a very kind way over green tea! This investor was a celebrity in the distressed investment space and had the reputation of being very aggressive. What he was saying was a very realistic assessment of our predicament and the conversation took place after the Draghi July speech.

From Tokyo, we took our flight to New York, arriving there in the evening. We were going to New York to participate in the New York Stock Exchange ("NYSE") Portugal Day on 15 October 2012. Most of the top executives at bigger Portuguese companies, some officials, journalists, PRs and investment bankers were there. We were there for the event, but as was to become our habit, we took advantage of the situation and planned to meet the maximum possible number of investors that were interested in meeting us.

The night we arrived, having just landed in New York, we had a drink in the bar before going to bed. One of the PR officers, who was part of the group, informed me that I was going to make the front page of the daily newspaper with the highest readership the next day. The subject would be my wage. The day after, an investment banker I knew warned me I was going to have problems due to my high wage. I guaranteed him that the wage was not as high as he was implying and he was relieved. Background noise...

These domestic issues did not take much of our attention. Next day, we had to be careful at the podium of the NYSE, when ringing the bell, not to be smashed against the wall by the enthusiasm in being part of the picture of a big Portuguese representation. The presentation in the NYSE was another very useful testing ground, even if investors were scarce. We used it to test the part of our presentation that focused on Portuguese exports make-up and performance. It was a very relevant testing ground as in the audience there were several representatives of exporting companies. Their reaction would be a very important sounding board to check if the story we were telling was really robust. They were very excited with our new perspective on the Portuguese economy. They had not seen it in that light but thought it made a lot of sense and bought into it.

One evening, we went over to Madison Avenue to meet one of the biggest US asset managers. We had in audience a group of very experienced investors in emerging markets, most of them managing money for the Private Clients division of the banking group. We faced a barrage of questions on the numbers for the Portuguese economy. They questioned us on all the figures they were expecting us to keep on the top of our minds. I remember clearly making an effort to remember the number describing assets of the banking sector as a percentage of GDP. They were just testing us and it was very useful. During the next few years, I would keep all these numbers updated in my mind and some of them I still do. I would make a daily effort to memorize the relevant figures and would test myself constantly during the day.

In the NYSE, we received a visit from an investor that had already come to see us in the office during the summer. We met him with the State Secretary to the Prime Minister, who was also participating in the event and which the investor had also visited previously. He was the investment manager of a smaller bond fund, with a higher risk profile, and looking into sovereign situations similar to the one of Portugal at the time. He was part of a big US asset management house, the first non-hedge fund US investor that had shown interest in buying our bonds. He was very knowledgeable; he had a PhD in economics from one of the top US universities. He was interested in discussing the latest government proposal that had created a massive negative popular reaction. The protests against this new policy had been so widespread that the government had to back pedal on its implementation. The policy the government had proposed consisted in the reduction of the employers' contribution to the social security counterbalanced by the increase in the employees' contribution. The motivation was to try and replicate a currency depreciation in Portugal by reducing the labor costs faced by corporations. The investor was visibly shocked with the lack of justification for a measure of this kind and was questioning us. "Come on, Joao, you are a Chicago economist. You know that a measure like this should be irrelevant." He questioned the State Secretary on why the government decided to move ahead with such an idea. His rationale, as an economist, was that independently of who would pay for the contribution the economic impact would always be the same. With competition for workers, which you would expect to take place in the exporting sector, corporates would increase wages to compensate for the increase in the workers' social security contributions and offset the positive impact of the policy on labor costs. As long as the overall sum of the parts was neutral, you would expect any impact to be null. But, socially, the perception was awful. This was too high a price to pay for a measure with no expected impact, at a time when austerity was already biting. He was looking at me, waiting for my nod. His rationale was similar to the one used in the irrelevance theorem developed by Modigliani and Miller, and the latter was in Chicago when I was doing my PhD. I avoided making any comment and just smiled.

That same night we had a dinner with hedge fund managers somewhere in Greenwich Village. They were really convinced that Draghi's July announcement and the European Central Bank's ("ECB") follow-up Outright Monetary Transactions ("OMT") proposal would be aimed first at Portugal and Spain. This would mean that Portugal could, according to them, be one of the first beneficiaries of this new policy. Portugal was reforming and complying with an adjustment program which was a necessary condition to become a candidate for OMT. They mentioned there would be more investors with the same view at the time and said this could be a good time to restart government bond international issuances.

On the way back to the hotel, in discussion between ourselves, we were convinced that it would be quite dangerous to issue at a time when the market could have built this type of convictions. We could issue successfully based on a speculative view on what the ECB was going to do at our own risk. The demand for Portuguese bonds would be driven by these market views, but would this be sustainable? If following the acquisition of bonds investors were disappointed by the lack of ECB action in the context of the OMT, they would try to sell back the bonds to the market, a market still lacking participants in size and diversity, and the price of the bonds would suffer. This would just make the Portuguese bond market less attractive for new bond buyers and reverse the increase in stability, or decrease in volatility, which was making the bonds gradually more desirable for investors. To rush into the market based on fragile beliefs could harm the work that we had been doing: to restore Portugal's credibility based on the merits of its policies and economic structure. This was an effort to be continued through time. As I mentioned before, we were not interested in "touch and go" transactions but wanted to establish the foundations of a regular market presence based on a sustained recovery in the perception that investors built on the Portuguese situation.

Our first trips to London, Tokyo and New York inaugurated a period where we would be constantly on the road meeting investors. We would come to the US at least twice a year, to the UK once a quarter and to France, the Netherlands, Germany and the Nordics twice a year, occasionally visiting Spain, Italy, Belgium and Austria. Each time, we would tend to schedule four to five meetings a day with investors. During these trips, we focused on many different themes. Some were prevalent throughout those years, while some were specific to the stage of the adjustment process Portugal was going through.

A theme we have already mentioned and that was an important part of our communication strategy was the Portuguese export performance. As explained previously, we decided to include it in our presentation in response to a portfolio manager's challenge in a presentation trial I had done just before joining the IGCP. The export story provided the "hope" part of our pitch to investors, pointing toward the first growth signals during the period of GDP correction that characterized the beginning of the adjustment program. When we started our investor visits, there was a generalized lack of knowledge about the Portuguese economy. Worse, there were some negative stereotypes spread by some in the press: the idea that Portugal's exports were concentrated in traditional sectors like textiles and agriculture and based on cheap labor. As we have seen in the previous chapter, in reality Portuguese exports were diversified in terms of sectors, with electronics and machinery providing an important share. Portuguese exports were integrated in the European industrial value chain and had been migrating upward in terms of value added. The industry had survived the shock of the European integration of Eastern European countries and China's accession to the World Trade Organization but had to transform itself as a response. Tourism played a role too, but the main message was one of resilient diversity. In addition, Portugal was, during this period, increasing its exports of cars to China, mainly Volkswagens produced in the south of the country. A good chunk of the big exporters were linked to the car industry. Textiles and agriculture were much less important but still played a relevant part, as did chemicals. During our conversations with investors we spent a good amount of time going through the numbers and discussing the most recent export growth numbers, including the sectoral and geographical contributions. These changed during the years, as when the European economy contracted, exports to Europe underperformed exports to the rest of the world. The fact that Portuguese exports were still growing while Spanish demand was contracting made our point on resilience stronger. In the opposite direction, when the rest of the world exports contributed less to growth, European demand started to recover. When industrial exports slowed other sectors grew, including tourism, demonstrating to investors the importance of sectoral diversity. As part of our presentations and in order to provide some color to the pitch, we started to include more and more examples of exporting companies and sectors. The IMF Markets Department that looked into our presentations rightly insisted on the importance of including export case studies.

After having left the IGCP, at the beginning of 2015, I felt our effort of spreading knowledge on the Portuguese export sectors was vindicated. At the time, I was having breakfast in London with an investor with whom we had various conversations during the previous years. When I mentioned that I thought investors were not giving enough credit to Greece's adjustment process, he said that Greece was not comparable to Portugal. One of the reasons he provided for his remark was that Greece lacked a diversified economy that could work as a robust export engine driving growth. I doubt this investor would have said this in 2012 when we were having our first encounters with current and prospective investors.

Not all investors believed that the adjustment in Portuguese external accounts was sustainable. In our visits to Paris we always met with very experienced economists that provided technical support and analysis to the investment committees of the institutions that invested in Portugal. In our tours of the city we visited more insurance companies than anywhere else but also visited some asset managers. Most of the former, maybe even all of them, were reluctant holders of Portuguese bonds. The bonds were a legacy of their investments prior to the European sovereign crisis. Some of them were still sellers of the bonds each time an opportunity arose. Our job, in their case, was to convince them it was worthwhile to stick to their bonds. In the latter case, there was one asset manager of a different kind, with more flexibility to invest according to fundamentals, with a larger mandate from his investors. This asset manager was an early supporter of our bonds and maintained a strong interest throughout the process of rebuilding market access. Each meeting we had in their offices, which were really beautiful offices, was very dry. We always felt that we were sitting for questioning in a police station. To emphasize the analogy, they took notes of everything we said. It looked as though they were preparing a report, which they probably were, to be distributed by the members of the investment committee. We always ended the meeting asking them about their position on our bonds and appetite for more. They always answered in a matter of fact manner kindly showing us the door. But from our first issuance they were regularly present in the order books for the bonds, and we would always pay a visit when going through Paris. The insurance companies were also very technical but we never really saw them in our bond issuances investor lists. One of these economists working for an insurance company would argue somewhat aggressively that our adjustment in external accounts was a by-product of the recession, and when the economy recovered, Portugal would go back to external deficits. His point was that the austerity was depressing consumption, and consequently Portugal was importing fewer goods. When the economy recovered, consumption would pick up again and so would imports. He was really convinced that the external surplus was due to the fall in imports and that these would not be sustainable unless the economy stayed depressed. We tried very hard to explain to him that a good share of the adjustment in external accounts was due to the export performance and that this performance was here to stay. He was skeptical. Exports were showing such a good trend probably because Portuguese companies, unable to sell in a depressed domestic market, were dumping, in despair, their production at discounted prices in external markets. We explained to him that exports were growing across sectors and geographies. I believe we were not very successful in our efforts to convince him. Anyway, as a result of these discussions, we decided to include in our presentation one page on the contribution of exports as a percentage of the external adjustment in Portugal and in other countries of the periphery. As expected, Ireland was the most impressive case of an external adjustment driven by exports but Portugal came just after. As expected, in Greece the adjustment was mainly driven by the contraction in imports.

As regards dryness and directness, and in line with some stereotypes, it was difficult to beat some of our Dutch investors. Some of the more specialized funds, with mandates from their investors similar to the French asset manager mentioned previously, were some of our earliest supporters and were interested in buying our bonds in the market even before we had issued our first bond. But each time we visited, we were treated coldly, bombarded with questions, and our answers treated with some irony. And following the visit, these investors would come back and buy more bonds. I met for a beer much later in the process some of the tougher ones, when our bonds were trading at prices too high to be of interest for them, and they were very friendly, candidly confiding that their retirement dream was to open a bed and breakfast in the south of Portugal.

In September 2012, following the announcement of the reduction in the employers' social security contribution and simultaneous increase in the employees' contribution, Portugal saw some of the biggest demonstrations that the country had seen in the last 30 years, the most attended since the agitated post-revolutionary period at the end of the 1970s. Hundreds of thousands of people took to the streets to demonstrate against the Troika adjustment program. These huge, record-beating, crowds were broadcast around Europe. During the fall of 2012, when we met investors we had a lot of questions concerning the country's level of social cohesion. Investors knew perfectly well their history: a lot of these difficult economic adjustments failed due to popular pressure. In several countries, governments started correcting economic imbalances but eventually had to backtrack due to social pressure, reverting the initial effort in part if not in full. Investors want to understand if the process can be sustained until results become robust enough. If they believe the efforts will be quickly reversed, then they will not feel comfortable investing in the bonds as they risk losing part of their investments later on. During the process, most investors were worried about the sustainability of the reforms. They worried that the patient might die as a result of the treatment. A good amount would argue for a more moderate adjustment, concerned that a too deep adjustment could have to be reverted if it brought about too much popular suffering, putting at risk the healing of the Portuguese economic condition.

During that period, we spent a lot of time explaining social and economic conditions in Portugal—how the political system was anchored in two center parties, both historically pro-European. We showed the current composition of the Portuguese parliament in our presentation, discussed how it had evolved since the revolution in the 1970s and how the latest polls were looking. Some investors were quite interested in following the evolution in the polls of the most extreme parties. At the time, new parties were showing up in Europe and more extreme parties were experiencing strong advances in the polls in other countries. Investors were checking if similar patterns were taking place in Portugal, but the polls did not show any signs of that phenomenon in Portugal. Some would ask us about how solid the coalition in power was. It was only when investors started to be less worried about these issues, by the summer of 2013, that Portugal went through a political crisis sparked by a dispute within the coalition.

Regarding social conditions in Portugal, and in the context of our presentation that was leaning toward the analytical and intended to be fact based, we used to discuss the amount of days lost to strikes. In addition, investors inquired insistently about any repeats of the massive September demonstrations' numbers. When we looked to illustrate how generalized the demonstrations in September were, I used to mention that even my mother had participated in the anti-Troika September demonstrations, an unusual occupation for her. And sometimes, to lighten the discussion a bit, I would mention my nephew asking my mother at a weekend family lunch, with a confused expression, why my mother participated in demonstrations against her own son. Later, at a lunch in Lisbon, an American investor that became a good friend, asked in a round table: "Has your mother been to any demonstration lately?" to which most investors and colleagues present laughed heartily. I answered with a very decisive "no."

Political and social issues were approached in different ways depending on the geographical regions we were visiting. Germans and Swedes inquired if hatred of Angela Merkel and Germany was generalized in the population. We always answered citing the level of support in the population for European integration, which remained at a high level in Portugal throughout this period. In France, investors were surprised with the mildness of the social protests given that the Portuguese government had eliminated so many holidays. Some would mention that if that was done in France people would take to the streets and break a few shop windows.

We faced the most fundamental question in a roadshow in Belgium. The investment bank that had organized our trip had been unusually disorganized. They had forgotten to bring the printed presentations to the meetings. We had not brought copies ourselves with bad habits from all previous roadshows, expecting the bank salesman that was accompanying us to the investors to bring the print outs under his arm. But worst of all, the meeting was outside Brussels in a smaller city relatively far, and we did not have enough time between the meetings to make it punctually. And it was snowing quite a lot, which slowed us in the highway due to the lack of visibility. When we got to the meeting, the investor, which was an insurance company, was represented at the highest level with two board members attending. We barely had the time to discuss anything as we were risking not catching our plane back. To start the meeting I thought it would be better to be sincere and present our situation: "I am sorry we are late but the meetings were scheduled with a low knowledge of the Belgian geography and the heavy snow did not help. In addition, we are risking missing our plane back. We have ten, fifteen minutes, and thought it would be better to go directly to your questions." They did not hesitate and the Chief Investment Officer, after explaining that the investments in Portuguese bonds were guaranteeing their insurance policies, mentioned that their clients were mostly Belgian farmers who expected their policies to be safe. They explained they were invested in long-maturity Portuguese bonds and asked if we intended to pay back. I explained what the Portuguese government was doing with the objective of honoring all its commitments and the sacrifices that were being made by the population to balance the country's accounts. I am not sure if our lack of punctuality and rushed departure helped convincing them that the government of Portugal was intending to respect its commitments.

In Sweden, we had more difficulty in convincing investors on the feasibility of Portugal's efforts. In reality, Swedish investors never participated in our bond issuances in the two years in which I was at the IGCP. The reason was simple: Sweden had gone through a crisis at the start of the

1990s and had to go through an adjustment process similar to ours. They were convinced that what allowed them to achieve the correction was the fact that they had their own currency. Their currency's depreciation at the time had helped them. It had a positive impact on exports, which softened the blow of the recession. Since Portugal was part of the euro, it was lacking an important stabilization instrument. As a consequence, they expected our correction would have to be much more brutal and they did not expect Portugal to be able to go through such a process.

In France, we once had a very nice surprise. In one of our issuances in 2013, we noticed a French investor, that we believed to be quite conservative, purchasing our bonds. This was out of tune with the type of interest we were seeing in our bonds coming from France. We decided to include the investor in our next visit to Paris, where we were going with the State Secretary. When we got into the meeting, we were surprised to be greeted in Portuguese by one of the attendees. We quickly found out that the investment manager that helped convince the management committee to buy our bonds was Portuguese, the daughter of parents that had emigrated to France decades ago. She still had a house in the interior of Portugal where she would go regularly. She was very informed, technical and respected by her peers and seemed to have defended well the investment case in our bonds. It was the beginning of a relationship with an institution that was to become a stronger buyer of our bonds, an exception in France among investors of its type. Theirs was one of the phone calls we received when the government was about to fall during July 2013. They were worried and struggling to understand what was going on in Portugal.

Another big challenge, when going through the process of regaining market access for our bonds, was that during each stage of the process, defined by different yields on the bonds as demanded by investors, corresponding to different perceptions of country risk, different investors would be engaged. This was very nicely explained to the Minister of Finance by the Head of Fixed Income of one of the investment banks in a meeting organized by us in the Ministry. The objective of the meeting was to explain the process to the Minister by means of a very credible outsider.

During the first stage, when the price of our bonds was still very depressed and investors were anticipating default with a high probability, investors were trading the bonds based on their perception of how much they could recover on the bonds in case Portugal defaulted. This stage was in reality very brief and lasted not much longer than the first quarter of

2012. At this stage, only hedge funds interested in distressed credit would really be potential buyers of the bonds. They would have to check which negative scenarios the prices of the bonds were reflecting and whether they found those scenarios too pessimistic. For instance, in case there was a PSI, as happened in Greece, what would be their expectation of bond haircut and compare it with what was implicit on the price of the bonds.

This stage is followed by investors that are counting with a low probability of default on the bonds but have a mandate to handle risky situations. They invest in distressed borrowers if they are expecting them to recover and their yields to gradually normalize. They are expecting to take advantage of the bond price appreciation. When we got to this stage, we still had some hedge funds involved in the market, but some emerging markets funds came in and also some fixed income funds with a more flexible mandate.

Later on, investors that are looking to collect the yield on the bonds but are not expecting much variation in prices get involved. They are looking to get some premium in terms of return versus the bonds of countries in the north and central Europe. An example of these investors is the pension funds in Scandinavia.

The end of the process will be attained, as described by the investment banker that afternoon in the Ministry of Finance, when you manage to bring back the specialized government bond investors, focused on interest rates dynamics. At that stage, the credit quality of the country is no longer such a relevant consideration. The yields would have to be quite low and the market pretty stable. To get to that point will take time and will only be possible once the rating agencies upgraded Portugal above investment grade.

This was a summary of the path that Portugal would have to travel on its way back to the markets. If Portugal got further down this path, it would ensure that it could issue the sizes that were needed to satisfy the high financing needs of the state, including the bond repayments coming in the years ahead. The challenge of this exercise was that it consisted of a relay race. At each stage, new investors would have to relay the investors that had been involved at the previous stage. This meant that at each stage we would have to look to engage new investors in our bond market, with the extra challenge that part of the new demand was satisfied by investors that were selling in the secondary market. These were looking to realize their profits. Some of the most aggressive hedge funds that had bought our bonds during 2012 had no longer any interest in buying our bonds at a yield of "only" 5%. Not only that, some were willing to sell and look for the next highly distressed sovereign opportunity. In meetings with investors, we had multiple situations at the end of 2012, and mostly at the beginning of 2013, where they told us that our bonds were no longer "juicy" enough for them, meaning they needed to take more risk and get a higher return as per the mandate they had from their own investors.

It happened that investors at a given stage would inquire if investors with a profile that fitted the next stage were starting to come into our bond market. They were thinking aloud, in our presence, about how they could exit their investment. They were inquiring if we were already lining up the investors that would be willing to buy their bonds at a higher price and for a lower yield. They would ask us if we had been visiting pension funds, if those were starting to participate in our bond issuances, if we had been speaking to the rating agencies and if we had some visibility on the timing of future rating upgrades.

The focus on the rating agencies was justified by the fact that rating upgrades had the potential to bring new investors into our bonds. I remember a meeting in London with an European asset manager, specifically with the people responsible for investing their more flexible European bond fund, and they were explaining to us how they were estimating the time it would take for Portugal to reach back investment grade status. They proceeded to ask us if we thought their calculations made any sense.

It is interesting to note the important role more aggressive and flexible asset managers, part of the hedge fund community, played in the process of price stabilization of Portuguese bonds. Their impact was felt more substantially during 2012. By looking at the macroeconomic numbers, testing the quality and conviction of Portuguese public officials and checking the conditions on the ground, they were the ones that took a lot of risk when the prices of the bonds were very depressed. They were the first believers in our process. They played an important role during the peripheral bond recovery, buying the bonds when there was a lot of uncertainty, understandably expecting high returns on their investments. They started the relay race. Later on, a prominent financial journalist was writing an article on this positive role, which was counterintuitive to the public opinion given that these funds do not always have good press. He checked with us if his understanding of the importance of their role was correct and we confirmed.

Each roadshow was prepared very carefully in close partnership with our primary dealers. The primary dealers were the investment banks that gave support to our bonds in the market and would participate in transactions when we issued bonds. During the entire process, we worked very closely with the investment banks. They would assist us when we were deciding which regions to visit. They would then contact their clients in those regions and recommend a schedule of investor visits. Before the roadshow, we would discuss with them if the investors were the right ones to visit at this stage, if they fitted the objectives of this particular trip and if these investors were really interested in buying our bonds or just wanted to see us to fill some space in their geo-strategic analysis or just for intellectual curiosity. Given that we did not have a lot of time we were trying to keep our visits as focused as possible. This does not mean that we would not include the curious types too. They could always play a role by spreading our messages by word of mouth throughout the market. But the visit would have to include a strong core of investors either already involved in our bonds or thinking seriously of getting involved.

Then the bankers would follow us to almost all the meetings, sit there listening to our pitch, sometimes adding some clarification, and, in the end, would usually inquire about the interest these investors might have in our bonds. I say that they came to almost all the meetings because a few times they were asked to wait outside. They were always a bit offended when this happened. Once in California, in a meeting with an investor that was a long shot, a manager of a public endowment, when we were looking to increase the capillarity of our penetration into the US market, he dismissively asked the bankers to wait outside. When we came to the meeting he frankly acknowledged that he was not a fan of bankers.

As I have outlined in the list of challenges that we were facing, we needed to rebuild the investor base for Portuguese bonds. The previous buyers had experienced heavy losses in our bonds holdings and had been under pressure from their management and/or shareholders to reduce their exposure. Most were forced to sell the bonds during a period when prices were dropping fast. Remember the empty roadshow in Frankfurt with the State Secretary for Finance. We needed to find new investors.

As outlined in our initial plan, we intended to look for US investors with a more open mandate, probably including emerging markets bonds. We established contact with a lot of these investors during 2013, when we visited the US, both coasts, twice. These investors came to Portugal and some others had offices in London where we could meet their Europe-based economists. As a consequence of our success, as the prices of the bonds appreciated and the yields dropped, some of them started to lose interest. This happened in 2014. They had played a huge role during the intermediate stage of the investor relay race. Now, the time had come for funds with lower return targets and less risk appetite.

We were constantly looking for new targets. Not only did we need to rebuild the investor base but we also aimed at diversifying the investor base. To establish a solid and regular presence in the sovereign bond market we had to have a lot of investors involved, with different objectives, looking for different bond holding periods, from different geographies. The logic is very simple. If for some reason we are dependent on one group of investors located in a given region and those investors suffer a synchronized change in circumstances and they need to sell bonds, our bond prices will suffer. If we introduce diversity into our investor base, then this price drop will be perceived as a buying opportunity for other investors that are experiencing different circumstances. In consequence, bond price moves will be smoother. With a diversity of buyers, the market tends to be more stable in terms of price moves. In addition, if you want to issue bonds and are depending on a single investor base, and at that time they happen to be in a difficult spot, you will not be able to do it. If you have multiple investor types coming from a diversity of geographies, even if some are unable to participate in an issuance, others will be available. That was the problem that Greece had for a long time: it depended on a relatively small group of hedge funds to be able to issue bonds. They took a long time to get through the first stage of the relay race.

Diversification was the main reason why, since 2013, we spent so much time on planes. With this objective in mind, we would try to understand very carefully where other European peripheral sovereigns were placing their bonds. We were constantly trying to understand where Ireland and Spain were placing their bonds. At a given point in 2013, when looking at the geographies where Spain was having more success than ourselves, we penciled France, Germany and Scandinavia. In France and Germany, we believed they were attracting insurance companies that would not invest in Portugal, but we had not thought of Scandinavia until then. We asked some of our primary dealers about what they thought about our prospects in Scandinavia. None was very positive. We picked one, not an obvious choice, and asked her to organize meetings for us in Scandinavia. The bank came back to us a few weeks before the trip mentioning that she had not been very successful in building investor interest in the meetings. We said there was no problem and that we would pick another bank. They reacted promptly to the suggestion, telling us they wanted to do it and would try harder. We spent one day in Copenhagen, one day in Stockholm, half a day in Helsinki and half a day in Oslo. In Copenhagen, we met a few pension funds that became steady supporters of our bonds during the second and third stages of the relay race. The conversations there were very technical, very focused on the macroeconomics of the adjustment process. Our counterparts there were always sharp, very informed and challenging. They had been investing for a long time in Danish mortgage-backed securities and understood fixed income well. In Helsinki, we had a breakfast meeting with multiple investors as we were not an obvious source of interest for one-on-one meetings. We started our presentation in a too bullish manner. One of them quickly interrupted me asking if this was intended to be a BS marketing session. I responded immediately that we were there to talk about strengths but also weaknesses. If he wanted we could start with the risks and how the government was thinking of dealing with those. Their reaction was positive and they remained engaged throughout. A good share of them would become frequent participants in our bond issuances from 2013 onward, past the time I had left the IGCP. In Sweden, we met a few investors, from hedge funds to pension funds, with not a lot of success and with some skepticism as already described. While our team was working together at the IGCP, they were never relevant participants in our bond market. And we never came back. In Oslo we had a strange meeting, unexpected. We were prepared for a meeting with officials from one of the Ministries and in reality they were managing a pension fund that could be interested in our bonds. The meeting had come through official sources and not through the bank organizing the trip. We had prepared an official update on the Portuguese situation. They looked at us slightly surprised and said they were investors and wanted to listen to our entire presentation. The trip was a success, and on the following issuance we had a good participation on the part of Nordic investors. Their interest in our bonds only increased over time. We even received calls from the press asking us if the Nordic percentage of a new issue was due to the manager of the Sovereign Wealth Fund of Norway. For the Portuguese press this would have a lot of meaning: it would mean that our bonds were being stamped by one of the most respectable investors. Needless to say, we never commented on specific investors with the press.

During the last stage of our process, mostly in 2014, the big global asset managers, placing big orders for our bonds for a variety of their funds, started to play a role. Their participation was crucial to sustain the two big issues we launched in early 2014. Those transactions made Portugal's exit from the Troika program a reality.

When we saw the participants in our bond issuances, we could visualize most of them. We tried to understand what they wanted from our bonds. We had repeated interactions with them. Images and stories from previous encounters were frequently remembered with a smile. I can remember the case of a German investor, scheduled on a German roadshow, to whom Cristina gave some examples of the Portuguese footwear industry and how it was moving up the value chain. One of those designer shoes had been used at the Oscars ceremony. In their visit to Lisbon, the investor asked Cristina for the shops where she could buy the famous shoes. Cristina gave them the directions and we received a picture of the acquired shoes attached to an email from Germany. Like in any relationship, trust is important. Once when I had a call with an investor that used to speak to the Minister of Finance, I asked the Minister if he had any special indication for me regarding their previous meetings. He said, dismissively, to just tell them the truth about anything they need to know, "that is what I always do". At the IGCP, we always tried to present the situation in a candid, fact-based way, always alerting about the risks. Investors dislike unexpected surprises. They can deal with the risks as long as they are identified. They did not like the political instability in 2013 as they had not been warned that this could happen. We always tried to warn them of what could happen and we were deeply distressed by the fact that we did not anticipate the possibility of political instability in the government at that time. It was a mishap in the path of rebuilding credibility that could have cost Portugal very dearly.

References

1. IGCP. "Portugal: Moving Ahead, Investor Presentation." (January 2013).
2. IGCP. "Recent Developments in the Portuguese Economy and Government Debt Market." (11 January 2013).
3. The Associated Press. "Thousands Protest Austerity Measures in Spain and Portugal." New York Times, (September 15, 2012).
4. Donald Rumsfeld. "Press Conference by US Secretary of Defence". NATO Speeches. June 6, 2002 https://www.nato.int/docu/speech/2002/s020606g.htm

CHAPTER 4

International and Domestic Ecosystems

Abstract In this chapter I focus on the importance of the press and the rating agencies in our re-engagement with investors and the markets. The local press also proved more and more relevant as the support of the domestic public opinion proved an essential ingredient of a successful return to the international markets. I start by explaining the roles that are played in bond markets by different types of news outlets: the wires and the press. They play an important role in building consensus within the bond investor community. In consequence, it is crucial to have a proper communication strategy and it is very helpful to be assisted by professionals. Following each transaction, we looked to explain its rationale to the press. The rating agencies play a crucial role as investors skim through their reports looking for clues of their future rating actions. I emphasize the importance of managing the downside in the sovereign ratings. I illustrate the difference between Portugal and Ireland in what concerned the management of the rating agencies before 2012. I emphasize the importance of keeping an active dialogue and an open communication but also of arguing every decision.

Keywords Wires • Financial press • Communication strategy • Rating agency • Sovereign downgrades

J. M. Rato, *The European Debt Crisis*,
https://doi.org/10.1007/978-3-030-61174-3_4

The international press had an important role to play in the completion of our task. Investors are, as expected, wide readers of the international financial press and what is called the wires. The wires, as news providers such as Reuters and Bloomberg are called, are the most up-to-date distributors of information. As companies announce results, as the governor of a central bank delivers a speech and national statistics come out, the headlines show up in Bloomberg screens almost immediately. If you want to follow market action and receive market sensitive information as it comes out, the wires' screens will be just in front of you. If you value receiving news updates without much delay and being delivered a constant flow of information, you have your Bloomberg or Reuters screen close to your seat. Investors in sovereign bonds, as expected, like to receive the relevant information as soon as possible as they try to make sense of the market action. When they see prices of sovereign bonds moving, they like to be able to identify which piece of new information was behind the move. They can then evaluate if the change in price is justified by the news or not. As national statistics come out, for instance a new GDP growth number or the new level of budgetary deficit, the news is delivered to investors and to market makers (traders) via the wires. Then, some of the traders may want to adjust the prices at which they offer to sell or buy the bonds. The wires serve as the financial system's plumbing through which information flows are channeled to the different market players.

The following will illustrate how quickly the information flows through the wires. Once I came out of a conference in Lisbon on the theme of retail certificates for local investors. It was a very domestic set-up to discuss a theme mostly relevant for a domestic audience. As, at the time, the issue of market access was being followed very closely by the public opinion in Portugal, I was met by a barrage of questions from journalists as I was leaving the conference room. At the time, I was no longer a beginner and could easily answer the questions in a way that would not create any problems to us or the government and avoid negative headlines. I said a few generalities and repeated the messages that we were looking to convey to the markets at the time. Thirty minutes later, as I sat in my office, I could read in my Bloomberg screen what I had said to the journalist when leaving the conference. It came out first as a headline in a Portuguese digital financial newspaper where someone at Bloomberg picked it up. This serves as a good example of the immediacy of the news flow. This is why I learned to regulate spontaneity when speaking with journalists, mostly when met randomly.

The daily financial press, like the *Financial Times* or the *Wall Street Journal*, is not as much a provider of instantaneous news; these dailies provide more of a background reading and are used as a basis to form an opinion on a specific topic or, at least, to convey what is the current consensus around this topic. The weekly press plays a similar role and reflects even more what the most widespread views within the investment community are. The weeklies are read by a wide readership including finance professionals that like or need to follow financial, economic and political themes. They play a very important role in the establishment of a consensus. In that sense, they were very important to us. We strived to convince them of our messages as we did with investors. Our objective was that our messages would coalesce into a positive consensus, aligned with our beliefs of course. We were always very careful in evaluating the sustainability of our message. As I have mentioned before, Portugal would need to come repeatedly to investors in the next few years and we were striving to build credibility. A touch-and-go relationship with investors would not help us in any way to become independent in terms of funding from the Troika.

For example, when we started our work, I remember reading in one of the most relevant current affairs magazine editorial a description of Portugal's exports as still mostly concentrated in traditional sectors depending on cheap manpower. This was a false perception that we were to counter in our presentations to investors. It would save us a lot of effort if we could convince the press that the Portuguese exporting sector was richer in terms of composition, more integrated in the global value chain and in higher value added activities than in the past. We were working hard so that they started writing articles on Portugal with more emphasis on how diversified our exports were. Before this ever happened, we would have had to discuss the data with investors and wait for the word of mouth to spread. We would do the same regularly with the members of the press. We were very jealous when Spain managed to convince a major investment bank that it would become the new European industrial powerhouse. Of course the resulting piece of economic research, well grounded in evidence, made the rounds of the markets and ended up summarized in the press. It became a consensus view very quickly. We felt at the time a very swift change of sentiment toward Spain on the part of investors, who had been mostly skeptical previously.

When our team started at the Treasury and Debt Management Office for Portugal ("IGCP"), in June 2012, we agreed with the Minister of

Finance that we would speak to the foreign financial publications and wires but not to the local press. This made sense, as domestically the political situation was very fragile. The wrong headline could easily explode out of proportion. At the time, the Ministry of Finance had an outstanding contract with an international financial communication consultancy. We were asked if we were interested in keeping this contract as it was not being used by others in the government at that time. After analyzing what this company could offer us, we decided to tell the government it made sense to use its services. It would be too dangerous to approach the international press by ourselves without the kind of support the company could offer us. We needed to make sure we were speaking to the right people about the right topics and at the right time, that our counterparts were understanding our message. When we had a point to make or a message to convey, we needed to know what was the right channel to use. After choosing the right channel, we had to make sure our message was clear and not misleading—and, most of all, that we were quoted in the right way. This last point kept me awake at night multiple times. I would go to bed after a meeting at a newspaper in London and after reading and correcting the received quotes. And then I would worry if the corrections were properly made and if the quotes would have the right impact and would be properly contextualized. My heart would race when reading the article the next day, and I would only rest when I verified that everything was OK and after checking the first reactions to the article. In this process, the communications consultancy played the role of my guardian angel, following up through the whole process. Starting by agreeing the rules of engagement with journalists and then making sure they were respected. They made sure that I was interacting with journalists they trusted and that would not play tricks on me. They would also warn me of any idiosyncrasies beforehand.

Each time we completed a transaction in the debt markets, we tended to go to London to explain to the wires and to other financial publications what we were doing. It was important to keep the press informed of the path we were following and how the transaction that we had just completed fitted the sequence of our actions. We would explain what we were trying to do next. Our objective was to make our actions as predictable as we could and the most effective way to convey our plans to the investment world was through the press. So, after a few of those visits, we started to build a relationship with some of the journalists and they started to anticipate some of the explanations we were coming to give.

One of our main focuses with the press was to avoid, as much as we could, negative headlines linked to Portuguese government bonds and with our actions in the markets. Along with our communications consultancy we were always on the lookout for all the news that came out concerning the Portuguese government bonds.

All this effort did not mean that we did not suffer any mishaps. As, at the time, I had a lot of meetings, I allowed one especially dangerous situation to fall through the cracks: a meeting with a journalist from a Japanese news agency. By the time I found out whom I was speaking to in my office, it was too late. To make matters worse, the journalist barely spoke English and I was not sure he really understood what I was telling him. He recorded the conversation. Following this very awkward meeting, I rushed to the phone and called our communications consultancy. They had to contact the journalist and convince him to send the quotes before the text would be published. He agreed to do so. When I received the quotes, my worries were confirmed. It was clear that the entire conversation was misunderstood. I corrected the quotes and sent them back. Our communications consultancy called me that night, admonishing me not to repeat the mistake: "we prefer not to work over spilled milk." It was a fair admonition; they should have been in the loop and managing the situation for me from the beginning. They would have probably advised me against the conversation, at least in the format it took. If we had decided to move ahead, they would have pre-agreed the terms ex ante so that they could manage the process from start to end. And the nightmare did not end there. As the interview headlines came out in Japanese, they were poorly translated into the Bloomberg news feed and they did not sound good at all when they came to the screens. The communications consultancy had to contact Bloomberg to ensure that the translation was properly corrected. We prayed that the headline did not spend enough time on the screens to reverberate. We had escaped that time and could breathe more comfortably.

One of our first contacts with the press took place in Brussels, where we met the Brussels press attaché of a major newspaper at our communications consultancy's local offices. It was during the fall of 2012, just after the record-breaking demonstrations that took over Portugal in protest against the Troika program. The interviewer was quite insistent in asking me what was my perspective as a citizen, particularly considering the suffering of the Portuguese people as a result of the austerity measures that were being undertaken under the economic and financial adjustment plan. I told him that he was probably not interviewing as a regular Portuguese citizen but because I was heading the Debt Management Office and so he would understand if I would not share with him my private citizen views. At the end of the interview, he congratulated me, smiling, that in my first interview I did not fall into any of the traps that he had laid out for me during the conversation. I was quite surprised by how frank he was and thankful that he explained to me the risks in the game so early on in the process!

In one of our trips, we had other conversations with journalists where the difficult situation of the Portuguese people, with high levels of unemployment, particularly youth unemployment, and more and more families where both the members were out of work, came out. I remember once, in a group conversation, when a journalist asked me how I could be speaking so coldly about the situation when the people were suffering so much in my country due to some of the reforms that I was describing. I had to explain that we lived in the country and we experienced the popular suffering and anger, including from people very close to us, including the family. But we were there to describe our efforts and strategy to return to the bond markets so that Portugal could regain funding autonomy and would not have to go back to the Troika.

We tried to keep ourselves to a fact-based approach, as objective as possible. In London, with the Portuguese Ambassador and the State Secretary for Finance, we met for an off the record conversation with an important financial publication. They had a negative editorial view regarding the process Portugal was going through. They tended to group Portugal with Greece. They characterized the Portuguese economic situation as a vicious circle in which the adjustment was having a negative reinforced impact on growth, making it more difficult to reduce debt and to attract investor to our bonds in a sustainable way. On the opposite, they spoke highly of the Irish process which they offered as an example that Portugal was unable to follow. Their reasoning was linked to their conviction that Portugal would not have the capacity to come out of the crisis through the export sector as Ireland was doing. They were quite ironic in the way they dealt with the State Secretary's and the Ambassador's arguments to show that Portugal had exporting capacity. It was a very frustrating meeting.

A few months later, we had one of the journalists present in this London meeting in our offices in Lisbon. The State Secretary to the Prime Minister had organized the schedule and included us. We sat with the skeptical journalist and went through the export numbers for different sectors and export destinations. In addition we ran him through the State's financing tables. These tables showed all the projections for the State's financing needs for the next few years and how we intended to finance those needs. We spent a good hour or more peeking into tables and graphs. I believe the other visits he made during his stay went in the same direction. He mentioned he really appreciated the fact-based approach and that everyone was taking time to run him through the numbers to illustrate the Portuguese situation in such a degree of detail. Following this trip, we had the first of a series of more positive articles coming from that very widely read publication.

In line with our efforts to rebuild the Portuguese credibility, each time we did a roadshow, we informed our communications consultancy and tried to arrange for meetings with the press wherever we went. The resulting articles came out in very different languages and the communications consultancy would supply us with a translation.

Another important stakeholder in our path to return to the medium to long term bond markets was the rating agencies. Investors peered over every report they published, looking for clues of possible future actions. At the start of our mandate, investors were still worried about more downgrades that could trigger another bout of selling and bond price depreciation, pushing our road to restore normality further out. In addition, rating agencies play a really important role in the relay race described in the previous chapter. Investors buying the bonds currently, are expecting new investors to come in the future at higher prices to take up their positions. The steady re-engagement of investors would play a crucial role in the price stabilization and appreciation. To keep this momentum going, you need to expect rating upgrades sometime in the future. That is the reason why investors read the rating agencies' reports looking for positive signs, subtle changes in tone that could indicate that the rating perspective will move in the needed direction. In that sense, like in the case of the press, the rating agencies' reports work as a coordination mechanism, influencing the mainstream views within the investor community concerning the Portuguese developments.

As we have seen in the first chapter, the downgrades of 2011 and 2012, bringing the bonds to junk status, and in good part triggered by the Greek's Private Sector Involvement discussions, had a huge impact on bond prices due to investors' forced or panic sales. The issue with ratings is that they can come down very quickly but tend to be very slow on the way up. Ironically, the further down they drop below investment grade the longer and more difficult it will be for them to come back to investment grade status. And without the investment grade status, it is very difficult for some investors to engage back with the bonds.

Ireland maintained an investment grade rating with S&P and Fitch throughout the crisis; it stabilized on the downside at BBB+ for both. Only Moody's downgraded Ireland into junk territory, Ba1 in July 2011, close to when Portugal had been downgraded to Ba2, and with a similar justification: "following the end of the current EU/IMF support programme at year-end 2013 Ireland is likely to need further rounds of official financing before it can return to the private market, and the increased possibility that private sector creditor participation will be required as a precondition for such additional support, in line with recent EU government proposals." In the case of Ireland, Moody's presented the factors that stopped it from moving to a lower rating: "the downward pressure that this created is mitigated in Ireland's case by the strong commitment of the Irish government to fiscal consolidation and structural reforms, and by its success, so far, in achieving the fiscal adjustment required by the EU/IMF programme."[1] These arguments, as you can see, were highly subjective. How do you measure a "strong commitment"? And Moody's downgraded Portugal further to Ba3 in February 2012.

In the case of Fitch and S&P, Portugal was rated BBB- in the summer of 2011, which compares with the BBB+ status kept by Ireland. In November, Fitch had downgraded Portugal to BB+ and in January 2012 S&P downgraded it to BB whereas the Irish rating stayed put. These actions increased the upward effort needed for Portugal to recover a proper rating when compared with a much more favorable Irish situation. Ireland was kept in investment grade territory by two rating agencies, keeping its access to a wider investor base (most investors that can only invest with at least two investment grade ratings) that were now out of bounds for Portugal.

The rating agencies started to publish rating methodologies, but part of the rating is still driven by subjective evaluations. The final rating action is subject to a decision from a rating committee allocated to each sovereign to which that country's allocated analysts have to present their arguments.

When preparing to take a rating action, the accompanying report is sent beforehand for comments to the domestic institutions that are responsible for following the sovereign's rating. In our case we coordinated with the Ministry of Finance cabinet for the State's reaction to the draft reports.

[1] Moody's press release on Ireland rating action, 11 July 2011.

One alternative that can be very important in managing the rating process is the right to contest the arguments underlying the rating decision. This right is a very important tool available to manage the rating downside. It allows the sovereign's representative to argue that the downgrade is exaggerated. To contest a rating action you have to present strong arguments. Then the rating agency will have to consider your arguments at the level of the rating committee.

The reason we know this procedure works is that we participated the first time that Portugal contested a rating decision during the crisis. This would have been the last downgrade suffered by Portugal in 2012. We asked for a delay in the decision to downgrade. Our argument was that this action was based on a rationale that we believed would be proved wrong in light of the results of the next Troika program review. So, we requested a delay until the rating agency received all the information following the publication of the upcoming Troika review report. They accepted our argument, and waited, and then decided not to downgrade after receiving the new information. If they had not accepted our argument and went ahead with the downgrade, I firmly believed they would not have been able to upgrade us back as quickly and this could have reversed the positive dynamics our bonds were experiencing in the market. The decision to contest was mostly an initiative of one of the IGCP directors, who deserves most of the credit for it and probably should have received a medal for it. She showed us it pays to fight every corner when you have valid arguments. There were rumors that the Irish did the same when the rating agencies were pushing the ratings of European sovereigns down in a bout of panic. Using these procedures they may have been able to avoid some downgrades that would have left them in a more difficult position when managing their return to the bond markets. These rumors do not surprise me given the fighting spirit and technical capabilities of the Irish officials.

As far as I remember, we always had a conference call to discuss a draft of a report, as we engaged in the fight for every corner. These discussions were always supported and many times motivated by our economics department. The team would meet to coordinate which arguments to use and to choose our main areas of contention. Then we would call the rating agency at the pre-arranged time. I would walk the room backward and forward as I brandished our pre-selected questions and criticisms of what was written and how it was written. While I paced with the phone in my hand, four of five of my colleagues had their eyes fixed in me. We were all conscious of how important these moments could be. We were all in full fight back mode and living intensely the moment given to us to explain why the country was not in such a poor shape as the text was implying. Illustrating how subjective some of the rating agencies opinions can be, I remember that in one of the reports the rating agency mentioned their doubts that Portugal would not go back on some of the reforms. The way it was written could even suggest there was some cultural stereotype. So I contested the sentence. I asked what were the signs this would happen. Because I could not find them in the draft they sent through. Where were the facts on which they were grounding this sentence? I asked if I had any reason to suspect that this was based on stereotype. Because we were Portuguese, a people from the South of Europe, Latins? From the other side came complaints that of course this was not the case. They offered very quickly to remove the sentence from the final report. They agreed it was a very serious accusation to include in a report without proper substantiation.

As part of our efforts, we tried to keep an ongoing dialogue and, more than that, establish a stronger relationship with the rating agencies. When the teams came to Portugal, we tried to arrange for them to meet all the relevant people that could be useful for their assessments of the situation. As with investors, we stressed the point that we were always available to speak with them and to try to help in case they had any questions.

One of the rating agencies wished to speak to an ex-minister of finance that was voicing doubts concerning the economic adjustment process in Portugal. She disagreed with the policies that were being applied and believed they were generating too deep a recession. We had the contact of the ex-minister and arranged for the rating agency analysts to speak with her personally. Following the meeting, the rating officials, after having heard her arguments, went back convinced that the alternative she was proposing would be far worse for debt investors and that it was doubtful it would be achievable given the circumstances. They were thankful that we helped them speak to the other side of our arguments. The ex-minister was extremely courteous and called us to give feedback on the meeting.

Another time, they called complaining that they were not able to schedule a conversation with a government official. He would not answer their requests. I called the official and asked him why that was the case. He was afraid that the rating could be under review (which was not the case) and that if something happened his conversation could be blamed for a negative rating decision. I said I thought this particular risk was inexistent and that it was his duty to receive them. As he grumbled, I asked at what time he was available during the day when the rating agency was in town. He gave me an hour and I told him the meeting was confirmed.

In one of their visits, two rating agency analysts told us that they had a meeting scheduled at the communist workers union. They were a bit anxious about the reception that they would be given considering they worked for an American rating agency that was apologetic of the need for labor reforms in Portugal. I was curious with the outcome too, so during our next meeting I inquired how the visit went. They said it went very well, and the union leaders were real gentlemen and argued their points in a very peaceful and respectful way. In consequence, they said that they had strengthened their views that Portugal had a very robust institutional framework. The visit to the communist union had strengthened a positive view on the Portuguese institutions, which is a very relevant part of the sovereign rating methodology.

In each of our trips to London or New York, we tried to schedule a visit to the rating agencies for an update. In addition, we tried to meet as many members of the credit committee of each agency as possible so that they could hear from us about the situation in Portugal. It happened that we had long meetings with some veterans of sovereign rating, that were not that informed about Portugal. We would spend our time, guiding them through the crisis origins, the composition of parliament and the beginings of the existing political parties, gradually moving through the economy, the exports, the reforms, the fiscal adjustment, the banks, our strategy and so on.

As we explained at the beginning of this chapter, we had agreed with the Minister of Finance that we would not speak to the local press, focusing on the international one instead. This changed when the Minister of Finance changed. As we will see later, during 2013 there was a crisis in the government following one of our issuances and one of our US roadshows, making us see that we could not continue disconnected from the domestic reality. On one side, to do our job properly and map well the risks the investors were exposed to, we needed to increase our alertness to the domestic political situation. As mentioned previously, investors hate to be surprised by events that were never perceived as risks before. On another side, it was important that the domestic public opinion understood what was at stake on the debt management front. In some sense, they should be part of the effort and better understand what we were doing. In such a way, we could build a wider support base in Portugal.

I had been speaking to the press before. When the bond issuances took place in January and May 2013, I was assigned to one of the TV networks to explain what had just happened. In addition, I had already participated in two long interviews on TV, always with a pre-approval from the Ministry of Finance. I had no press coaching domestically, unlike the high level of support I got on the external front. I was always aware of the downside risks in terms of both the domestic politics and the possibility of being misquoted in the international press.

A specific episode provided me with another eye opener. I was surprised to read in a newspaper, in a piece related to the public sector companies swap portfolio renegotiation, an allusion linking the low discount that was offered on a swap unwind and the fact that I had worked for that bank in the recent past. It was very malicious. This swap was a standard swap and not a highly speculative and exotic one. So there was really no reason for a discount. In addition, I managed the conflicts of interest concerning this bank and had not participated in the process. I discussed the issue with someone I know and he asked me who the journalist was. He said the journalist concerned was a very decent person and he would arrange for us to meet. We then met for breakfast at a classic Portuguese breakfast spot near my home. I explained my background and what we were trying to achieve at the IGCP. I believe she understood where I was coming from and excused herself about the way she had presented the story in the newspaper. The fact was that this meeting worked and from then on she would call me to check if what she was thinking made sense. Even if she did not always correct her piece when I tried to explain she was wrong, she gave me the benefit of the doubt. I understood that it was better to reach out and build bridges than wait behind a moat.

In another situation, a journalist that was researching the swap renegotiations called me and asked if what she was writing made sense. I said it made literal sense but there were some more technical details to it. So, I offered her a visit to the IGCP so that we could give her a quick refresher on swaps, almost like a half morning introductory course delivered by our team member that was overlooking the pricing of the state-owned enterprises exotic swaps. She accepted happily and from then on we had a much deeper reporting on the swaps renegotiation process from her.

We also looked to engage in dialogue with some of the editors of the local financial press. We asked them to come to the IGCP. We told them that we thought they had a very important responsibility in informing the public about what was going on in the process of returning Portugal to the medium to long term bond markets. For that, we thought it was our duty to give them quality information. All this made sense given what was at stake, we explained. The importance of avoiding a second bailout. The policy freedom that market independence would provide us with. The austerity recipes that would be imposed in the context of another Troika program. We asked them if they would accept to be run through the same numbers that we were showing investors and rating agencies. They were keen. And that was what we tried to do: to explain to them the financing needs of the State in detail and how we were planning to find the funding to match these amounts, how much would the retail market, hopefully, represent, how much we would have to issue in the international bond market.

This constant dialogue that was maintained proved very useful. Its usefulness was clear when in March 2014 a group of notables, spanning a vast spectrum of tendencies from ex-ministers of finance from right wing governments to leaders of an opposition party from the radical left, issued a manifesto for the restructuring of the debt.[2] It came a bit late in the process as by that time we had mostly guaranteed the return to the bond markets. A good part of the measures they defended had been part of the successful negotiation by the Minister of Finance Vítor Gaspar in 2013. They were poorly informed and had a weak grasp of the numbers (at least some of them, some were probably comfortable with restructuring debt held by private investors and others were playing the political game). It was clear to an informed reader that to achieve their goals, their restructuring proposals would have to include private investors. The timing could not have been worse as Portugal had just issued twice successfully and was walking toward re-establishing market access like it existed before the crisis: a combination of syndicated new issues and auctions. I was happily surprised when I received calls from a few of the editors we had been talking to. They were preparing opinion pieces arguing against the logic of the manifesto. In the pieces they were reminding the public that the interest on the European loans had already been twice reduced and were aligned with the European cost of funding, and the maturities had already been extended during the previous year. There was no space for lower rates

[2] Published by the newspaper *Público* on 11 March 2014, as "Manifesto: Preparar a reestruturação da dívida para crescer sustentadamente."

unless they were to be subsidized by our European partners. So, any new extensions and interest reductions would have to affect private investors as the IMF would not accept any changes on their loans. And this would jeopardize investor support and would throw us toward a new Troika program involving more austerity. We were really proud that the financial journalists were embracing their role of serving the public in this way.

Too much exposure to the local press can bring its risks too, as it creates some enemies along the way. At a given point, we had the idea of bringing a journalist inside the IGCP to cover, in multiple articles, the different areas of the institution and to make it better known to the public. We arranged for the quotes to be pre-checked and we allowed all the heads of departments to explain their roles to the journalist. In consequence, we received some calls from other areas of the Ministry of Finance asking us what we wanted to obtain from all this publicity. We received a call from higher-up in the government asking us about a part of the journalist's text that suggested that we were telling investors a different version of the divergences between the government and the Constitutional Court than the government was telling domestically. We were clearly getting more and more exposed and taking more risks with our more proactive interactions with the local press.

References

1. Moody's investors services. "Rating Action: Moody's downgrades Ireland to Ba1; outlook remains negative." July 12, 2011. https://www.moodys.com/research/Moodys-downgrades-Ireland-to-Ba1-outlook-remains-negative?docid=PR_222257
2. "Manifesto: Preparar a reestruturação da dívida para crescer sustentadamente (na íntegra)." *Público*, (March 11, 2014)

CHAPTER 5

Restarting the Engines

Abstract This chapter describes the re-opening of bond markets for Portuguese issuances and how it was possible. The process is presented in the context of the European peripheral bond market conditions at the time. In January 2013, following a roadshow in the US, we tapped an existing bond and came back to the medium to long term debt markets. The bond increase had a 35% participation coming from the US, showing that our diversification strategy was starting to bear fruits. I explain how the primary and secondary markets for government bonds work and the role the investment banks play. I emphasize the importance of liquid secondary bond markets for competitive bond pricing and investor participation. The process was still fragile. To keep the secondary market stable, it was important to avoid negative headline news that could trigger selling pressure by investors. It was crucial that the situation in Portugal evolved in a predictable manner in order to avoid the bond price instability experienced during periods of panic selling.

Keywords Portuguese government bond issuances • Portugal returns to the markets • Liquidity • Primary dealers • Bond syndicated issuance • Secondary bond market

As we have seen in Chap. 2, in October 2012 we had executed our first big transaction: an exchange that showed the Troika that we could deal with

J. M. Rato, *The European Debt Crisis*,
https://doi.org/10.1007/978-3-030-61174-3_5

financing issues in a way they were not expecting. We solved the puzzle of how to deal with a first big bond repayment not covered by the Troika's cash. We achieved it through exchanging the bonds redeeming in 2013 with bonds to be repaid further into the future. At the same time, we started to provide an answer to one of the main concerns of investors: how to deal with the wall of bond redemptions that we had discussed over tea with an investor in the Imperial Hotel in Tokyo. If we could execute more transactions of this kind we would be able to extend into the future the bond redemptions and smoothen the repayment obligations' summits. If we faced on a given year a considerable amount of bond repayments, we could try and offer more bond exchanges to investors, exchanging old for new bonds that redeemed further out into the future. The 2012 fall transaction was also the first sign of re-engagement on the part of investors. The fact that they were willing to take Portuguese government bond risk for two more years indicated they were more comfortable with the risk of Portugal becoming another Greece. Investors were showing that they believed Portugal would be able to handle the situation at least during the two years following 2013. If not, they would not have accepted to exchange bonds that paid back in 2013 for bonds that paid back in 2015. Additionally, and very importantly, this transaction removed the urgency of our return to the markets. Before the exchange, investors knew we would have to issue bonds before September 2013 to survive, which made our situation more difficult. As you might expect, an issuer that is perceived to have to issue bonds as a matter of survival risks not to be offered the best pricing conditions. If a buyer thinks you really need to sell your house in a rush, he will not give you the best bid for it. The same happens in the bond market. The bond prices will suffer if you are not perceived to be in a comfortable position.

Following this transaction, we were perceived to be in a comfortable position, as we had funding for more than one year. We had time to manage our return to the bond market with no urgency. On 3 October 2012, a Reuters article title was "Portugal buys breathing space with bond swap." The article started by saying that "Portugal returned to bond markets on Wednesday for the first time since a bailout last year, swapping short for longer-dated debt to buy time to fix its public finances." It proceeded by stating that "the swap will make Portugal's debt repayments easier next year, giving it time to make savings necessary for reducing debt and get the economy growing again so it can avoid a Greek-style restructuring."[1]

Even so, ten-year yields on Portuguese government bonds were still at 8.9%. As we have discussed in Chap. 2, the Portuguese ten-year yields were close to 13% in March and had already traded below 10% briefly in June. The downward pressure on yields continued following a momentum that existed already before Draghi's July announcement. Our debt exchange transaction helped reinforce this trend. By December 2012, the ten-year yields were hovering around 7%. In contrast Greek yields had come down massively but only following the Draghi announcement, approaching 10%.

The Irish process of restoring market access for their medium and long term bonds had started earlier than the Portuguese. Yields had been coming down since the fall of 2011. As we have seen in the previous chapter, it helped that Ireland managed to avoid the group downgrades that affected many European sovereigns at the beginning of 2012 and that the official European loans granted by the European Financial Stabilization Fund and the European Financial Stability Mechanism to Ireland had their maturities extended. Ireland was more advanced in terms of their economic stabilization process since it had agreed to a financial support program in November 2010, roughly five months before Portugal. During 2012, it was already showing positive signs as it was meeting the Troika targets. Ireland was a few steps ahead of us and we were always observing closely what it was doing. And, of course, as its process was working well, we only had to gain from being compared to the Irish in the debt markets. Our process was perceived to be somewhere between the Irish and the Greeks. When things were not going well, we would be asked to justify why we were not like Greece, and when things went well, investors would say that we were just following a similar process to the Irish. On 5 October when answering a Reuters question, I was quoted: "the strategy consists in attracting more investors and volumes back into our secondary markets and optimizing our bond curve, following a strategy similar to Ireland's."[2] As an interesting historical counterfactual, we could conjecture about what would have happened if Portugal had asked for assistance before it did—if it had requested for assistance at the start of 2011. Would we have

[1] Reuters Business News, October 3, 2012.

[2] Reuters UK Top News, October 5, 2012, "Portugal in debt strategy roadshows, no placements planned yet".

avoided some of the rating agencies' downgrades of early 2012 like Ireland? Would the yields have spiked earlier and at less extreme depressed levels for bond prices? Would a better starting point make our work easier? We would probably be seeing the positive signs of stabilization from the external account earlier in the process and would be in a stronger shape when the talks of the Greece Private Sector Involvement ("PSI") started to dominate the debate around Europe.

Ireland also started its activities in the market with an exchange. But their exchange took place in January 2012, when the Portuguese sovereign yields were peaking. They exchanged €3.53 billion of an outstanding 2014 bond for a new 2015 bond. They did it in order "to address the challenging funding cliff in January 2014, where almost €12 billion of debt was due to mature one month after the end of the Troika programme."[3] Ireland continued following this strategy by offering in July 2012 an exchange of 2013 and 2014 bonds into an October 2017 bond and an October 2020 bond. Notice that it was now able to execute these switches further into the future into bonds with five- and eight-year maturities. It managed to exchange €1.04 billion but mostly was able to raise new money for these bonds: €4.19 billion. Ireland had come back to the medium and long term bond market with new issuance. By the end of 2013, yields on ten-year Irish government bonds had already crossed 5%.

By January 2013, the Portuguese ten-year yields were close to 6% and the five-year yields were close to 5%. On 3 January, a Thursday, I received a call from António Borges asking me why we were not issuing bonds at this level. I told him that the year was just starting and this was not yet a good timing to issue. I believed we would have the opportunity to issue in good conditions soon. We arranged for lunch to discuss. I understood that António was conveying some sense of political restlessness. As discussed in Chap. 3, the fall of 2012 had seen an increase in social protest following the proposed change in the social security contributions by employees and employers. In addition, the budget exercise had been difficult, and the Minister of Finance, to accommodate for a deeper recession and the Constitutional Court's refusal to allow the continuation of some of the public sector remuneration cuts, had to announce a massive increase in taxes. Our successful returns to the markets would show to the population that the Troika program was achieving something. It would give the

[3] See "Accessing sovereign markets – the recent experiences of Ireland, Portugal, Spain, and Cyprus", ESM Discussion Paper Series / 2.

government the possibility to deliver some results at a moment when unemployment was very high, some of the unemployed were losing access to the subsidies and the population was very anxious about the possibility of more cuts.

At lunch, I explained to António that, at the Treasury and Debt Management Office for Portugal ("IGCP"), we knew we were expected to deliver a transaction and we were looking for the good timing. I asked him to trust us and we would deliver. I tried to protect the institution from the political pressure as much as I could and António understood that.

At the beginning of January, we were planning a roadshow in the US. By mid-January, we flew with the State Secretary for Finance Maria Luis Albuquerque to Los Angeles. We spent a day there, met four investors, travelling the monotonous and jammed highways between the different spots. San Francisco followed. There we met three or four more investors and then took the red-eye plane (overnight) to Boston. There was a thunderstorm and we had to land in New York, flying back to Boston later in the morning. There we met three other investors and flew back to New York. The State Secretary showed us she had a bottomless supply of energy as she endured three to five presentations a day with overnight flights and kept the stamina and the positive energy, always willing to answer all the questions. We were surprised how well informed about us investors were and about how technical the discussions could become. It made sense as one of the reasons we were targeting this investor base, with a long experience in emerging markets investments, was exactly because we thought they would understand better than others the story we were coming to tell. They had good returns out of macroeconomic recovery stories like our own. In some places, the asset manager's top management, that had a deep recollection of the Mexican recovery following the Tequila crisis, was attending the meetings. They remembered perfectly the different stages which these countries went through and were expecting us to go through similar processes. They proceeded to explain in a terse way what was awaiting us. In New York, we had a very well attended breakfast where the State Secretary presented the macroeconomic adjustment process, the budgetary measures approved for 2013 and the structural reforms Portugal was implementing. We would complement the presentations with our market access strategy.

After returning from our roadshow, in the week of January 21, we had built quite a strong momentum in the US. The last meetings we had in

New York were with investors that were actively involved in our bonds and interested in building bigger positions.

The investment banks that had not participated in the roadshow were quite careful regarding the possibility of issuing at that time and the members of our technical team that had not travelled with us were advising us to wait. But, at that point, it was clear to Cristina, Sofia and me that we had to move ahead and issue. So, we did. We decided that it was too early in the process to issue a new bond, so we decided that what made sense was to tap (increase the amount of) an existing bond with a five-year maturity. We were going to issue the bond using a syndicate of banks. We announced that we had mandated a group of banks to gather potential interest in the bond we were increasing in size. This took place on Tuesday, 22 January, in the afternoon. The idea was to assess if there was enough interest before moving ahead with the transaction. We would then kick off the process during the next morning. The fact that we were targeting US investors played a role due to the different time zones. US investors would have the US afternoon to express their interest to the banks. If our reading of the momentum we gathered in our US roadshow was right, we would wake up the next morning with a good share of the transaction already covered by the orders coming from the other side of the ocean. It worked: next morning we had more than 30% of our planned issuance covered by orders coming from the US. At that point all the banks felt comfortable with the transaction and were advising us to move ahead. The order book, the list of all the bond orders coming from investors, showed there was interest for €12 billion of bonds. It included orders from close to 300 different investors that had transmitted their interests to the banks. In the end, the team, as advised by the banks, decided to increase the bond by €2.5 billion and allocate the orders in a way that attributed to US investors 34% of the total, the highest ever, and by far, in a Portuguese government bond issuance up to that day. The October 2017 bond increase came at a yield of 4.891%. This bond had first been issued in 2007 as a ten-year bond with a yield close to 4.35%. At that point, Portugal ten-year yields were trading at 5.82%, coming from close to 7% one month earlier.

The government was ecstatic; it followed the transaction nervously during the day and we had to negotiate hard during the morning to get to a size of €2.5 billion after having pre-agreed to a size of €2 billion. The government still thought the deal was expensive. Given the demand for the bonds, we thought it made sense to do a bit more of size, allowing us to start to build a larger cash buffer. The political crisis that Portugal experienced later on that year would justify this slightly higher cash accumulation. Later in the day, as we closed the bond to more orders and announced the final size, the bond tap yield relative to the Bund yield, we started to receive some pressure from the Ministry of Finance for a version of the press release. Before writing the press release we needed to decide how to distribute the bonds between the investors that had shown interest. At that stage, the banks that participated in the issuance were agreeing on a distribution proposal so that they could come back to us for final adjustments and approval. Only after agreeing on the distribution of bonds would we close the final price depending on where the Bund reference was transacting in the market. All this takes time and delays the process of drafting and then finalizing the press release that had to include the final terms of the transaction. But the government was focused on the press release to be able to start the well-deserved media victory lap. Its nervousness was difficult to manage, as the bond distribution was particularly difficult to agree on that day.

The distribution of bonds between investors is a very important exercise and one of the main benefits of issuing bonds using a syndicate of banks. The issuance of new bonds or the increase in size of existing bonds is called, in debt markets jargon, the primary market. In the primary market the transaction takes place between the issuer of the bonds, the seller, and the investors, the buyers. The secondary market is where the transaction of bonds occurs between investors that act as sellers of the bonds and other investors, and in some case the issuers, that act as buyers. The reason why deciding on the distribution of bonds issued using a syndicate of banks is so important is that it influences the behavior of the bonds in the secondary market following the issuance. If the issuer places too many bonds in the primary market with investors that are just looking for a quick profit and to sell the bonds soon after the bonds start trading in the secondary market, then there will be too many investors selling and the price of the bonds will fall. This can create some instability in the bond prices and make it more difficult, and expensive, to sell bonds the next time you come back to the primary market. As you should expect, most investors are quite sensitive to the bond price performance in the secondary market following the issuance in the primary market. They are not happy if they lose value in their bond holdings just after buying them.

Another important criterion when the issuer decides to whom it allocates the bond to is the diversification of its investor base. If the bonds are only placed with the same type of investors and the investors are too homogeneous, you will tend to see less trading in the secondary market and an increase in the risk that too many investors may want to sell at the same time, creating higher price swings. When deciding to which investors you want to sell the bonds in the primary market, you are thinking about the diversity of your investor base. In consequence, the issuer can indirectly influence the stability of bond prices in the market. More price stability will attract more investors to the primary market the next time you issue.

As an alternative to syndicated issuances, where you have some control on whom you place the bonds with, an issuer can sell bonds using an auction mechanism. In the case of the auctions, the investment banks that are eligible to participate, called in our case (and usually) the primary dealers, bring bond orders to the auction at a given price without disclosing who are the final clients that have an interest in buying the bonds. During the auction, the issuer orders the investor requests for bonds by the price each one is willing to pay. Then the issuer checks the amount of orders that accumulate higher than a given price, the lowest price she is willing to receive for the bonds or the lowest price that allows her to place her desired bond size. This price is called the cutoff price. If the issuer uses a single price mechanism, it means she sells all the bonds to investors at the same price (the cutoff price) independently if they brought in orders at the cutoff price or above. The issuer then sells all the bonds at the cutoff price, which is the lowest price at which orders are satisfied. If the issuer decides to use a multiple price mechanism, she sells bonds to each investor at the price they brought the order to the auction. In this case, she sells bonds at multiple prices but all prices above the cutoff price. As you can easily conclude, the issuer is blind on the type of investors that come into the auction and to whom bonds are allocated, as the orders come in through the primary dealers and are automatically allocated. As opposed to what happens in a bond syndication, in an auction the issuer has no choice on how to allocate bonds.

Before the crisis, the IGCP followed a very monotonous and predictable process in the primary market during the year. It would issue one or two new bonds using a syndicate of banks. It would then, during the year, in a regular fashion, always at a pre-announced date of the month, increase the size of some of the existing bonds through the auction mechanism. Sometimes this auction window would not be used, usually in the summer and at the end of the year when the financial needs for the year had already been satisfied. The syndicates were bigger in size, €2–3 billion usually, than the auctions, €750 million to €1 billion. The bond increases were repeated until the bonds assumed a big enough size to ensure they were used as benchmarks, references for that given maturity date. This mega bonds would then allow for enough action to occur around the bonds in the secondary market as they allowed for a diverse investor base. When the Outright Monetary Transaction was announced following Draghi's July 2012 speech, eligibility to the program was linked to the access of the sovereign to the medium and long term bond market. In the fall of 2012, investors would ask us a lot about how we thought the European Central Bank ("ECB") defined market access. We would answer that we did not know with certainty but that for us to restore market access was to restore the same type of market access we had before the crisis. We thought this should be acceptable to the ECB. Saying so we were setting a clear objective for ourselves: not only did we have to restore our presence in the primary market by issuing bonds through syndicates but we would also have to restore regular auction schedules.

The primary dealer system that allowed banks access to transactions had been built at the IGCP based on very clear criteria. An investment bank had to present its candidacy to become primary dealer and then would start a trial period during which its behavior and performance would be tested. It would be tested based on different criteria. A very important one was the level of support that the primary dealer provided to bond trading in the secondary markets. They had to act as market makers in the bonds.

A market maker helps the functioning of the bond market by keeping stocks of bonds. The fact that the market maker keeps bond inventories allows him to commit to buy or sell bonds at any time for a given amount and at a given price. The market maker will post prices for buying and selling bonds and volumes on the trading platforms. For instance, it makes markets for €1 million of bonds for a price of €99 at which to buy, called the bid, and €101 at which to sell, called the offer. If an investor comes in and sells €1 million of bonds she does it for €99. Then the trader at the market making bank keeps the bonds, waiting for a buyer to come and take the bonds away. Without a market maker, a broker would have received the order to sell and would have to wait until a buyer for the same amount and at the same price (or higher) comes by. It would take more time. The market maker is said to provide liquidity to the market, making the bonds more liquid—liquid in the sense that an investor can sell the bonds faster and buy them faster at the screen prices or on the phone. If the market maker shows in the screens the same bid and offer prices but for a higher size, for example €10 million, you can say the market is more liquid. It means that an investor can sell immediately at €99 more bonds, up to €10 million in face value, consistent with what the market maker is posting on the trading platform screens. The seller just presses a button and executes the trade. Alternatively, when the market maker is only guaranteeing a bid for €1 MM and the investor comes in and sells €1 million of bonds, the market making bank can immediately correct its bid to €98 for the next €1 million of bonds. If the seller wants to sell €10 million, he will have to do it by executing €1 million trades each time at possibly worst prices. He risks that the market maker stops making markets after a certain point or at least adjusts the price down each time. In this case, the market is less liquid; it is harder for investors to sell back bonds.

By now, you may have concluded that the more buyers and sellers are active in a market every day, the easier it is for the market makers to provide liquidity to the markets. If a seller comes in and the market maker only expects a buyer to show up in one week, it will tend to be more conservative on the sizes and bid prices it shows for the bonds. In a diverse market, it will expect buyers to come in sooner and take it out of the bonds. Then it will be willing to make markets for bigger sizes and tighter differences between bid and offer prices.

You have to remember that it costs market makers to keep inventories of bonds. The bid-ask spread allows the market maker to be compensated for its costs. It is the difference between the price at which it buys bonds in the market and the one at which it sells those bonds. How many hours a day the market maker is available is also an important factor for a liquid market. If the market maker only provides markets for the bonds in the morning, it means the market is less liquid in the afternoon as an investor will have to wait until the next morning to be able to sell its bonds.

The extra carrot that will be provided to the market maker is to make it eligible to participate in syndicated issues where fees are paid by the issuer. Many issuers only consider well-behaved market makers, primary dealers, to be chosen to participate in syndicated bond issuances. Normally, to be part of that select group you have to be placed on probation for one year so that you can prove you are up to your obligations as a proficient market maker. Other obligations of the primary dealers include the provision of information regarding secondary market conditions. The primary dealers are the eyes of the IGCP into the secondary market for bonds. They provide information that allows the IGCP to assess if the market is liquid or not. At the IGCP you rotate bond issuance between the compliant primary dealers but give priority to the better ones, as ranked according to previously disclosed performance measures. Each year the IGCP organizes a lunch gathering for primary dealers when each one's ranking is disclosed individually and privately. As expected, the lowest ranked tend to argue their punctuation in each of the considered criteria. The lunch that follows is a good opportunity to restore harmony.

Liquidity is very important for investors as there may be a need to sell all or part of the bonds as circumstances change and investors need to adjust their portfolios. If it takes them two weeks to sell back €100 million of bonds, and cost them more in terms of price versus what they see in the screens, they will consider buying lower volumes of bonds in the first place. They will be less conservative if they know they could sell back bonds faster and with less cost. In addition, investors will demand a liquidity premium on the yield of the bonds (or a discount in the price) for less liquid bonds. This is why the presence of good market makers or primary dealers in the market for bonds is very important for an issuer. During our process of re-assessing the medium and long term markets for bonds, besides the positive pricing momentum, we were looking to generate a positive liquidity momentum. At the start of our process, primary dealers were pretty much inactive in the secondary market for our bonds. Given the moves in price they were seeing and the constant presence of headline risks in Europe, notably surrounding the Greek PSI, it was out of the question for the investment banks to keep portfolios of our bonds in inventory. They risked a sharp reduction in value from one day to the other and there were long periods without any buyers showing up. During periods of stress, sellers would come in clusters and primary dealers would risk extreme and quick accumulations of bonds. In addition, at the beginning of 2012, investment bank shareholders were keen to see the investment banks reduce their exposure to the government bonds of countries in the periphery of Europe. In consequence, at the start of our mandate at the IGCP the level of compliance of primary dealers with their obligations was very low. We worked closely with our primary dealers during 2012, 2013 and 2014 to re-establish some normality in the secondary market. Only from January 2014, the volumes in the secondary markets, considering both the over the counter (executed on the phone) and the platforms, recovered to levels significantly higher than the ones observed since January 2011. In January 2012 bid-ask spreads for ten-year bonds quoted in Bloomberg were close to 7 percentage points, meaning that if you sold back a bond immediately after buying it you would lose 7% of bond face value (from 90 to 83, for example). On January 2013, the bid-ask spread on the same bonds would be close to 1.5 percentage points. A big change!

To keep the secondary market stable and the primary dealers calm, it was important to avoid headline news that would provoke selling pressure by investors. This would make the primary dealers retract from the market and bid-ask differences to get wider. Investors would become more cautious when buying our bonds and engage in smaller sizes. The process was still fragile in 2013. It was crucial that the situation in Portugal evolved in a predictable manner in order to avoid the bond price instability of periods with one-sided selling. This is why we had to explain very clearly where we were going: the restoration of full market access as Portugal experienced before the crisis. For the same reason, it was important to avoid unexpected negative events on the domestic policy front. Even bad news should have been ideally identified as ex ante risks. But, as we will see later, surprises were on the way.

References

1. Axel Bugge and Andrei Khalip. “Portugal buys breathing space with bond swap.” Reuters Business News, (October 3, 2012).
2. Rolf Strauch, Juan Rojas, Frank O Connor, Cristina Casalinho, Pablo de Ramon-Laca Clausen and Phaedon Kalozois. “Accessing Sovereign Markets – The Recent Experiences of Ireland, Portugal, Spain, and Cyprus.” *European Stability Mechanism Working Paper Series/*2 (June 2016).
3. Andrei Khalip. “Portugal in Debt Strategy Roadshows, no placements planned yet.” Reuters UK Top News, (October 5, 2012).
4. Association for Financial Markets in Europe. “European Primary Dealers Handbook”, as updated Q4 in (2015).
5. IGCP. “EUR 2.5 Bn OT Syndicated Tap due 16 October 2017.” Press Release. (January 23, 2013).

CHAPTER 6

Bumps on the Road

Abstract In this chapter I describe the spring and the summer of 2013 when Portugal went from issuing again a new long-term bond and extending the maturities of its European official loans to a political crisis that threatened to jeopardize our work and bring the sovereign back to the situation of 2012. The situation in the Portuguese government bond market is placed in the context of the evolution of that in Ireland and Greece. In May 2013, Portugal issued a new ten-year bond. It was able to attract more conservative investors to its bond market and to continue to diversify investor participation. But it was still facing a wall of redemptions for the next few years. This still conditioned the type of market access available for Portugal. European support, in the form of the maturity extension of official loans, was crucial to smoothen the redemption profile and to potentiate future investor involvement in the Portuguese bond market. A political crisis during the summer of 2013 risks jeopardizing our efforts for a market-based exit from the Troika program. This chapter describes how bond market conditions were dragged into the domestic political situation.

Keywords European official loans maturity extension • EFSF • EFSM • Greece's debt crisis • Ireland's exit from Troika program

J. M. Rato, *The European Debt Crisis*,
https://doi.org/10.1007/978-3-030-61174-3_6

Around April 2013, we had our first roadshow in the Nordics, a new frontier we were exploring in our effort to rebuild the investor base for Portuguese bonds. As we have seen in Chap. 3, we were doing it mostly out of instinct, as the investment banks, our primary dealers, were not great believers in the potential of this market. In May, we went back to the primary markets to hit another milestone in our process: to issue a new bond. The January transaction had consisted of increasing the size of an existing bond. We were now going to issue a new bond and we were focusing on a longer maturity: ten years.

We believed it was expected from us, in order to show market access, to prove our capacity to issue bonds for maturities up to ten years. We had to demonstrate that investors were comfortable to buy longer term bonds again. Bonds of higher maturity have a higher price sensitivity to changes in the sovereign yield. Investors engage with longer maturities only when they are more comfortable with the risk. This would provide our European partners, incarnated under the institutional form of the European Stability Mechanism (the "ESM"), always the most skeptical observers of our achievements in the markets, a signal that we were moving ahead in terms of attracting investors and completing every milestone in the relay race mentioned in Chap. 3.

Since January 2013 we had been catching up very fast with Ireland in terms of milestones. The first bond syndication for Ireland after losing access to the market, not considering the bond exchange offering that took place in August 2012, was a tap of an existing five-year bond and took place in January 2013, just as it was the case for Portugal. The difference was that Ireland issued with a yield of 3.32% and Portugal did so at 4.89%, as we have seen in the previous chapter. They followed this transaction by issuing a new ten-year bond in March. The yield for this new bond was 4.15%. Portuguese ten-year yields were still close to the 6% where they had been since the January 2013 bond tap. At these levels, it would be difficult to issue bonds. We had to wait until May 2013 to follow Ireland on this one.

On the other hand, Greece's yields were still very volatile and were close to 10%, indicating that issuing bonds was pretty much impossible even if the bonds were trading much less depressed than in 2012. The debt restructuring that took place had alleviated the situation in the short term. The second Troika program for Greece was moving ahead through its first reviews. In April 2013, the second review had just been completed with a positive tone. But discussions that Greece would have to leave the euro were still re-surfacing from time to time as the country was still very much dependent on the Troika for funding and the economy was still very badly depressed.

In the beginning of May, we continued to play catch up with Ireland. Portugal issued a new ten-year bond at a yield of 5.67%, which still compared poorly with Ireland but anyway constituted an achievement that took us time to repeat; only in January 2014 would we come back to the primary market. The issue size was €3 billion for a total order book of €10 billion. The bonds were distributed widely between different geographies, which indicated that our strategy of rebuilding an investor base was really starting to bear fruits: 27% of bonds were placed with UK investors, which included mainly some of the biggest US asset managers through their European headquarters located in London, some specialized debt funds and some hedge funds; 16% was placed with US investors, mainly some of the most emerging markets focused investment funds we had been courting in our roadshows and who had been visiting us with some regularity. Following the Portuguese investors closely, which received 14% of the bonds, came the Scandinavian investors with 10% of the bonds. The effort of introducing these investors to our roadshow schedules, contrary to the advice that our primary dealers were giving us, paid off. We had sold close to €300 million of bonds to Scandinavian investors, Danish, Finnish and Norwegian. Close to the Scandinavian came the French with 10% of the bond issuance; Italy and Central Europe came next both with 7% of the bonds placed, areas where we had been less active if you exclude our regular visits to Germany. Only after those geographies did Spain follow with 4%. As you can see, we had managed to achieve an interesting investor diversification with our roadshows and we could easily identify most of the big investors we had in the book, as we had regular interactions with most of them. And we had started our effort to reach out, with constant travelling, barely more than six months ago.

We were also making progress on our investor relay race. Asset managers represented 51% of the bonds we had placed. Of course, these were a diverse crowd in itself, from emerging markets funds to credit funds and government bond funds with a more flexible mandate. Hedge funds only represented 7% of placed bonds and we had placed 6% of the bonds with central banks/sovereign wealth funds. Insurance companies and pension funds represented now 12% of the bonds placed. This showed we were managing to transition from more opportunistic investors to a more buy and hold crowd. The old investors were finding buyers in the secondary markets for the bonds they had bought at higher yields/lower prices and were able to realize their profits.

If you compare Portugal's May 2013 ten-year bond placement with investors with the Irish ten-year bond placed in March of the same year, you can find a very similar investor base. UK investors represented 25% of the bonds, very similar to the Portuguese bond investor composition. Scandinavian investors represented 12%, French 11% and US 9%. You can clearly identify less US investors, which made sense since a good chunk of them had an emerging markets focus and the Irish bonds' lower yields were starting to make them lose interest. Alternatively, they were starting to attract more investors from Central Europe, with 18%. These tend to be more conservative and rating sensitive. Remember that Ireland contrary to Portugal had an investment grade rating at the time. This may also be the explanation for a higher share of insurance companies and pension funds in the case of Ireland, with a share of 16% of the placed bonds. Asset managers, with a 52% representation, bought a share of the overall issuance similar to the one in our bond. Of course, at the Treasury and Debt Management Office for Portugal ("IGCP"), at the time we would meticulously perform this type of comparative exercise. We would look to check if our strategy was working and for clues regarding what should be the next steps to take. We always referred extensively to these pies, representing the investor participation, in our dialogues with investors, rating agencies, the international press and, also, with the official European institutions that tended to downplay a bit our achievements.

In line with the conversations we had with investors during the fall of 2012, including our conversation with an experienced distressed bond investor in Tokyo over green tea, we were still facing a very big challenge in the short term. We were still facing huge amounts of repayments for bonds and to the official institutions that had lent to Portugal under the financial and economic stability program: the IMF, the European Financial Stability Fund ("EFSF") and the European Financial Stability Mechanism ("EFSM"). The climb was steep: in 2014 there were close to €14 billion of bond repayments coming due, in 2015 more than €16 billion, including the first amount owed to the EFSF of just over €1 billion, in 2016 close to €20 billion, of which close to €7 billion owed to the EFSF and the EFSM. To keep it in perspective, we had just issued €5.5 billion in the first half of the year; it could be realistic to expect another issuance and maybe an extra exchange, but at the time it looked difficult for investors to see how we could deal with much more than €10 billion a year through issuances and bond exchanges. Portugal still had cash to receive from the Troika up to 2014, but in 2016 it would have to face up to €20 billion in repayments, which looked pretty difficult to satisfy through the available market instruments. It was a major perceived obstacle to the Portuguese market access sustainability.

In view of these difficulties, Portugal and Ireland were negotiating with our European partners a maturity extension of the EFSF and EFSM loans. They represented an important share of the 2016 obligations and transferring these to the future would make a big difference. This process took place during the spring of 2013 and involved the presentation of proposals by the Finance Ministries of Portugal and Ireland to the Eurogroup. Both Ministries requested the technical assistance of their respective Debt Management Offices. And as both Debt Management Offices had a very good working relationship, we exchanged views regularly between us. Our job was to propose a working extension of EFSF and EFSM loan maturities and justify it in light of the positive impact it would have in terms of the sustainability of market access for the sovereign bonds of both countries.

On 12 April 2013, when a Eurogroup meeting approved the ESM support for the adjustment program for Cyprus, it was decided to explore the possibility of an improvement in the loan conditions for Ireland and Portugal. The EFSF and the EFSM were very different institutions. The EFSM was created for the European Commission to provide assistance to countries in difficulty in 2010. It was financed through bonds issued on behalf of the European Union. Its support came from European Union member countries including the ones that were not part of the euro, like the Swedes and the British, and its implementing powers rested with the European Council. The EFSM closed the financing for each loan tranche given to a country on a back-to-back basis in the market (with liabilities that had the same maturities as the loans it financed). So each financing package corresponded to specific loan tranches. The EFSF depended only on the Eurozone countries and it financed its loans through a combination of debt that was issued with different maturities. The EFSF is a credit-enhanced vehicle where the assets are loans to countries under assistance and manages actively and dynamically its liabilities contrary to the EFSM. Its structure gives the EFSF more flexibility in choosing its own financing mix as it does not have to engage in back-to-back transactions like the EFSM, allowing it to manage maturity mismatches between its assets, the loans to sovereigns, and its liabilities. The EFSF was incorporated by the 16 countries sharing the euro in 2010. These debts were guaranteed by the Eurozone countries on a pro rata basis, in accordance with their share in the paid-in capital of the European Central Bank. The EFSF could then commit to extend the maturity of a given loan as it wished. However, the EFSM, which had each tranche locked with a specific back-to-back financing package, could only indicate an intention to refinance with a given maturity when the loan and its corresponding liability matured. That intention would always depend on the market conditions at the time of refinancing.

The Council of Ministers would have to agree on any average maturity extension. Then the Portuguese and the Irish Debt Management Offices would have to agree with the EFSF and the EFSM to which new or intended maturities each loan would extend.

On 21 June 2013, the European Union Finance Ministries gave the green light to a maturity extension of up to seven years of the average maturity of the loans provided to Portugal and Ireland. At the time of the announcement, Klaus Regling, CEO of the EFSF, said: "The extension will smoothen the debt redemption profile of Ireland and Portugal and lower their refinancing needs in the post-programme period. It will enhance the confidence of market participants and thus protect Ireland and Portugal from refinancing risks."[1] For sure, the extension was crucial in allowing us to achieve the market exit from the program, as the financing needs we were facing in the near term seemed now much more doable under the current market conditions. Our European partners had helped us in smoothening the wall of redemptions and sorting out the problem that had been pointed out to us in Tokyo the year before. The extension of maturities of the European official loans set us up for what we were going to do. It made it more possible. It increased our chances. And, I believe Portugal owes this chance, including being paired with Ireland at that time, to the work of its Finance Minister, Vítor Gaspar, and to his credibility with his partners in Europe. He played a crucial role, including diplomatically, in taking Portugal back from the hole it had dig itself into since the 1990s. I had, at the time, a very strong sense that our European partners were still not fully convinced that we were in a sustainable path out of the program. Alternatively, they seemed to be convinced in what concerned Ireland. And I believe his credibility played a very important

[1] EFSF extends loan maturities for Ireland and Portugal, press Release ESM 24/06/2013.

role in convincing our partners that the government in Portugal was serious and that the adjustment process was sustainable.

In March 2013, S&P reviewed the outlook on the Portuguese BB rating from negative to stable. We were quite enthusiastic about it at the time as it showed to everyone that Portugal was going through a positive momentum. There had been not so much of a tightening of our yields following the announcement, but up to May our bonds were trading with more liquidity and the secondary market was relatively stable. The May issuance came on the back of this period and yields were now tighter.

This positive trend that was gradually taking our bond trading environment to normality would not last. During the month of May, when the maturity extension was being agreed, I received a call which I had already received in the past. At this time, the call left me more agitated than before. The State Secretary called me on a Sunday checking on how much cash did we have in our accounts. That was a sign that something was happening in the political front. It indicated that the survival of the current government was at risk. I was flabbergasted: we were just planning to issue bonds and complete the yield curve with a ten-year bond. This would threaten all our efforts and surely destroy the positive momentum we had been experiencing in the market. I received the call from a plane that was close to taking off, so there was not much time for detailed explanations about what was going on. After informing the State Secretary for Finance about the amount of cash (more than €8 billion at the time) in the vaults, I called a minister with whom I had a good relationship and asked him what was going on. I explained to him that we had just issued bonds and it would not be a good time to surprise investors with a political crisis. This could send back our process of rebuilding market access to the point we were in one year ago. He asked me if I had a working contact in the CDS/PP, the political party, the minority partner in the government coalition. I had to think about it carefully and then I followed up with a call to a high-placed member of the party (CDS/PP) that was not at the government at the time but was very close to the leader of the party. I called him, explaining why I was so worried about the timing of a political crisis. We arranged to meet for a drink in a Lisbon hotel in the afternoon. I knew that in the meantime the cabinet was meeting to discuss. I was relieved when my contact called back before our meeting time: he said we could still have our meeting in the hotel, but he had good news; the cabinet meeting did result in agreement and a political crisis was averted.

Looking back with hindsight, this was only a first warning shot. But at the time we thought the issue had been sorted out. Actually on 5 May, the leader of the CDS, Paulo Portas, had gathered the press to announce that his party opposed a tax on pensions that was being negotiated with the Troika. He mentioned he would assist the Prime Minister to look for alternative policies. Now we can suspect that this was a sign that the tensions within the government, between the Minister of Foreign Affairs, Paulo Portas, and the Minister of Finance, were growing.

In the end of June we organized a roadshow in the US with an investment bank, one of our primary dealers. The request was quite straightforward: we wanted to increase the capillarity of our penetration in the US market. We were aware that the emerging markets funds were losing interest in Ireland as the yields edged lower. We wanted to look for new investors in the US. We would visit some of the investors we knew already but add to the trip insurance companies, mid-range asset managers in areas where we had not been like Chicago and Philadelphia, and high net worth divisions of global banks. We spent the entire week in the US—Cristina, myself and the organizing investment bank debt capital markets professional. We ended the roadshow in California. In Los Angeles, as I was on my way to visit an asset manager, a friend of mine that worked as an interest rate strategist at an investment bank sent me a message asking what I was doing in LA. He told me I was just about to follow his meeting with the same investor. Later on, we came across him at another investor's office where I could see him in the meeting room next to mine. Small world!

We landed back in Lisbon on a Saturday, and on Monday whatever had been brewing in the background since May finally came to the surface. The Minister of Finance resigned and wrote a resignation letter that was not amazing for the government. At the IGCP, we were livid. We had just come back from a roadshow with investors. We had no clue this was going to happen and we were looking like idiots. We had trouble explaining to the investment banker that had travelled with us what the hell was going on. We decided that we should email all meeting participants of the previous week's roadshow and make ourselves available for a conference call where we would explain what was going on as best as we could. Everything was pointing toward a solution that would ensure a smooth transition: the previous State Secretary for Finance, who most investors knew and liked, would take over as a successor to the Finance Minister.

I would have to go to the parliament the next day for my first audience concerning the state-owned enterprises swap portfolio renegotiation.

I was quite agitated by the end of the day, so I decided to go for a run to calm down. During the run, I received a call from my friend, the interest rate strategist that had been visiting the same clients during the previous week in LA. He had asked someone to translate the Minister's letter of resignation and had read it in a very negative way. He thought the letter was questioning the leadership capabilities of the current Prime Minister. I told him that I did not know much more than the letter itself.

On the next day, I went to the parliament. I went through the usual discourse from the radical left party, reminding viewers that I had been at an investment bank which, according to them, had helped fudge the Greek accounts and that I was linked in some way to the Lehman bankruptcy because I worked there. Then, when the second round of questions was coming closer, I saw the CDS MPs getting into a bit of an agitation, some of them leaving the room, and my phone started to buzz with calls. The left-wing MP then ironically mentioned it would be difficult for her to concentrate on her questions as the Minister of Foreign Affairs (from the CDS) had just resigned and the government was going to fall. That was the way I learnt what was going on, in a parliament audience, live on the parliament TV. I could not believe it! I was saved by the fact that the MPs still present were no longer interested in the topic I came to discuss and the session ended in an unusually fast forward fashion.

Now, we had a big problem. Investors would want to know what was going on. I was pretty sure that they were not expecting this, as much as we did not! One of the first calls I received was from a US investor, the one we had been interacting with regularly since the summer of 2012. He was quite nice, as he looked to be most worried about myself: "Joao, what are you thinking of doing next?" When I asked him what he meant, he said, "the government will fall, there will be elections, the anti-Troika left leaning parties will win and you will have to move on. What would you like to do next?" I explained to him that even if this was the right scenario, the center-left Socialist Party was a pro-European party and I believed would avoid confronting our European partners. We always reminded investors that the Socialist Party had played a crucial role in Portugal's accession to the European Union.

That Tuesday evening the Prime Minister spoke to the country. He refused to resign and promised to do everything within his reach so that the country could return to political stability. He said he would not accept the resignation of Paulo Portas, the leader of the government's minority partner, mentioning he thought an agreement could still be reached. "I will not resign. I will not abandon my country." As a small consolation to our challenges, he mentioned he had been caught by surprise by the resignation, which he was not expecting the day before. He added, "With me as a prime minister, the country will not choose the political, economic and social collapse. The alternative would be to discard two years of effort, ignoring all the sacrifices the Portuguese people have done and the signs of economic inflexion that are starting to appear."[2]

In the following days, the chairman of the European division of one of the US investment banks visited us. He wanted to convey he was not happy about the way the swap negotiation went through but, at the same time, wanted to move on in what concerned the relationship. He was supposed to meet the Minister of Finance. We went to meet her; she had been nominated but in practice the government was in a limbo. It was a strange meeting as it was not obvious where things were going at the time. She conducted the meeting with a lot of dignity that was appreciated by the investment bankers, but she did not have a lot to say.

On 3 July, the following day, Deloitte organized a gala to handle the 2013 Investor Relations and Governance Awards, where the IGCP was to be handed a prize. The gala had a strong attendance of executives and even some shareholders were present. As I came in, and was having a drink outside, trying to enjoy a nice Lisbon summer evening, I was approached by one of the members of a family that owned a few important companies in Portugal. He wanted to express his unhappiness regarding what had just happened on the political front, and he was mostly reproaching the behavior of the Minister of Foreign Affairs. One of his companies was looking at a possible transaction, which he said was made possible due to our work. And now everything was on hold. He mentioned he was very annoyed that political tactics were spoiling what had been achieved. At that point I understood that there would be an immense amount of pressure on the leader of the junior partner in the coalition to come back to government.

We used to comment between ourselves that for the first time in the recent history of Portugal, politicians were starting to get their actions marked to market. The public opinion and the corporate sector seemed willing to punish politicians whose actions had a negative impact on bond prices. What was happening in the political front was not a good thing but at least it made the public opinion more aware of the markets' sensitivity to political turmoil and how fragile the work of regaining market access

[2] *Público*, 2 July 2013.

was. That had been possible first and foremost by the policy measures taken by the government and the efforts made by the Portuguese people and then by our work on the ground, and was now in jeopardy.

In the end, a compromise was reached between the two parties in view of forming a new government. For this solution to be effective, the new cabinet would need the acceptance of the President. On 10 July 2013, the President refused to accept changes in the government but also to call for early elections before June 2014. He asked the three main parties to reach a compromise of "national salvation," a medium-term agreement between the political parties occupying the centre of the political spectrum.

Before the President delivered this message through a press conference, I had received a strange call on my mobile when I was in my office. A very formal voice introduced himself as the Secretary General to the President and asked me to keep the line free as the President would be calling me in the next ten minutes. I was quite surprised but said yes and he hanged up. I was still measuring in my head the chances that this had been a prank call when I received another call. It was the President. Again, I was not quite sure this was not a friend trying to be funny. The President asked me a few technical questions about the one year ahead financial rule followed by the IMF, current market conditions and how I thought the market could react to different scenarios. They were all very much to the point questions and I answered them in a straightforward manner. The call was short. I was well impressed as all the questions made a lot of sense given the situation.

The day following the President's communication I received a call from a friend. He was asking me what the President's speech meant. How would I explain it to the international press? "What does this national salvation mean? It looks like a coup in the Congo!" I calmed him down and tried to explain the events.

Following the President's press conference, we made ourselves available for calls with investors to try to rationalize what was going on. We aimed, as usual, to be as analytical as possible and we drew up the different possible political scenarios for the near future in a very rational manner. We made sure that investors understood we were not turning our back to the difficulties and were available to speak with whoever wanted to understand the situation better. I believe our availability during the crisis was very well perceived by investors and allowed us to gain some credits for later on in the process. Investors understood we were going through a difficult period in our job but that we felt a duty to keep the communication channel open at all times.

The market for long term bonds suffered during this period as you might expect. The month of June had already been quite poor, following a good performance in May on the back of our ten-year bond issuance. On 31 May, the ten-year bonds were trading at 5.55% yield. By 1 July, the bonds were trading at 6.34%, a yield at which it would be difficult for us to repeat the May transaction. By 12 July, the ten-year yields were at 7.42%. Most worrisome of all, by 1 July, the difference between the five-year yields and the two-year yields was 1.84%, with the two-year yields at 3.29%, whereas on 12 July, the same difference was close to 0.55% and the two-year yields were at 5.49%. In 11 days the two year had shot up by more than 2 percentage points or, alternatively, by close to 67%. The two-year yields had gone up by much more than the five-year yields, which was a worrisome omen for investors. It showed that investors were perceiving higher risks of default in the short term. Investors in Portuguese government bonds were once again considering more seriously credit risk. We were still far from the distressed levels of the beginning of 2012, but the markets were demanding more compensation for taking the Portuguese credit risk in the next two years. This was different from what was observed before the summer when investors were focusing on the medium to long term prospects for the sovereign. We had a few calls from investors and from the IMF regarding this move in the yield curve. A French investor called to ask what our perception was regarding this move and if we were expecting it to continue. The IMF representative came by and asked the same question (his office was a few floors above ours).

On 12 July, to make matters worse, the leader of the opposition Socialist Party called in the parliament for a debt restructuring; this probably explains in good measure why the yields peaked that day. On that day we agreed at the IGCP that it made sense to do some pedagogical work with the opposition party. Soon thereafter we contacted one of the party members responsible for fiscal issues. In our first meeting, I explained to him how we were telling investors that his party was pro-European. Was I wrong? I explained to them in detail how we had thought about the market strategy and the benefits we were expecting it to bring to the country. I have to say, that with time, they played a patriotic role by moderating their speech, mostly when meeting investors. Because as we felt the need to reach out to them, so did investors. A few months later, the leader of the opposition party gave a speech at the

London School of Economics. Following that speech, I visited investors in London. One of them, an economist for a big US asset manager, had gone to listen to him. We inquired how it had been. The investor told us it was pretty standard. The opposition leader had said all the "right things" and the investor had come back quite comfortable. We left the meeting quite comfortable too.

In the meantime, we also had to deal with the press. We were quite frustrated at the IGCP when on one of these days in the middle of July we read an article in one of the financial newspapers that brought back a theme that had been absent for most of the previous year: the possibility of a Greek style Private Sector Involvement in Portugal. The article included two fear-mongering quotes, one from a big asset manager that was not a big owner of our bonds and probably did not own many bonds in the periphery of Europe, contrary to some of his main competitors, and the other from an economic analyst from a second-tier investment bank that was known for some maverick views. This article came out on a week day. It was important that it did not spill into the press's weekend editions, not to spread this theme again. We called our communications advisory company and explained the issue. They thought it was a good idea to call one of the editors that was responsible for the section where the article had been published. We did so. I told him I thought it was not appropriate to write an article arguing such an extreme scenario based on only two opinions, from an asset manager that was not invested in our bonds and from an idiosyncratic economics analyst. I thought it would make sense to include at least more views. He only answered that it was a fair point and hang up with a very English "point taken." I do not know if it was our call but the theme did not surface again and, as far as I can remember, these two quote providers never showed up again in the context of news on Portugal.

By 1 August, the President had to agree on the new cabinet coming out of the old coalition of parties, as the compromise solution to involve the three main moderate parties in the parliament went nowhere. Portugal's ten-year yields were back at 6.33% and the two-year yields were at 3.38%, close to where they had been on 1 July. But even if the yields had gone back to levels before the political crisis, investors kept the memory of a very volatile July. Some of them sold when they thought the political crisis would mark the end of the adjustment process and condemn any chance of market access in the near future. Others had been scared by a period of wild swings in the market value of their position in Portuguese bonds. It was more difficult for them to convince their investment committees that Portuguese bonds were normalizing as they showed the recent graph with wild swings in the bonds price. The market has some memory and we would have to work hard to regain the confidence of investors. It did not help that during the summer, another negative decision from the Constitutional Court, regarding the reversion of wage cuts in the public sector, was announced. Was this decision the end of the line for the adjustment process, leaving no alternatives for the existing government? By mid-September, ten-year yields were back to yields close to 7.10% and two-year yields close to 5.5%. We had a difficult time ahead of us. Portugal would leave the adjustment program by April next year and we needed to restore confidence in our bond markets. We had barely more than six months to achieve it.

References

1. IGCP. "€3 Billion 5.65% OT due 15 February 2024." Final Press Points. (May 7, 2013).
2. Rolf Strauch, Juan Rojas, Frank O Connor, Cristina Casalinho, Pablo de Ramon-Laca Clausen and Phaedon Kalozois. "Accessing Sovereign Markets – The Recent Experiences of Ireland, Portugal, Spain, and Cyprus." *European Stability Mechanism Working Paper Series/*2 (June 2016).
3. European Stability Mechanism. "EFSF Extends Loan Maturities for Ireland and Portugal." Press Release. June 24, (2013).
4. Council of The European Union. "Council Extends Maturities of EFSM loans to Ireland, Portugal." Press Release. (June 21, 2013).
5. IGCP. "Notes from the 7th Review of the Economic Adjustment Programme." (March 27, 2013).
6. Leonete Botelho. "Passos não se demite, nem aceitou ainda a demissão de Portas." *Público*, (July 2, 2013).
7. International Monetary Fund. "Portugal, Seventh Review." (June 2013).

CHAPTER 7

Final Push

Abstract In this chapter I describe the process we followed as we approached the end of the program, which was the moment of truth when our strategy would be evaluated. If we were able to solidly establish our market access it would be a success; any other outcome could have very dire consequences to the Portuguese economy. During the fall of 2013, our situation was fragile. Investors were again concerned with the possibility of a Public Sector Involvement in Portugal. The domestic political situation was not completely settled as the confrontation between the government and the Constitutional Court was increasing in tone. To build a virtuous circle in the Portuguese government bond market and avoid a vicious one, it was important to attract a critical mass of investors. To achieve this objective, we planned a succession of transactions that brought us to a situation where Portuguese bond markets were experiencing a strong positive momentum. We executed another bond exchange in December, followed by two new issues in January and February 2014. We had turned around the situation: a clean exit through the markets was now on the cards.

Keywords Portugal clean exit • Bond market access • Bond exchange • Eurozone debt crisis • Sovereign liquidity buffer

J. M. Rato, *The European Debt Crisis*,
https://doi.org/10.1007/978-3-030-61174-3_7

During the fall of 2013, the fate of the Portuguese adjustment was undecided. The bonds were still trading at a relatively high interest rate (yield) in the market. The summer had seen the return of very volatile trading conditions. The bond issued in May had experienced a rough patch. Some investors were disappointed.

I recall a specific event in October 2013 that shows how fragile the process of re-assessing the markets was still at the time. As it frequently happened, we were invited by a European investment bank to present to a group of investors. The group included close to 20 investors and was very diverse. There were two pension funds from Holland, a big American asset manager and an asset manager from Finland. They sat in a room in one of Lisbon's top hotels during the day waiting for different people to present to them. Public officials like us, some opinion leaders and journalists were part of the day's menu. When our turn came, I remember quite vividly being asked again questions regarding the possibility of a bond haircut. Investors believed This could happen if in six months we were not able to restore a robust and durable access to the international bond markets. It was reminiscent of the questions that were brought up in similar meetings more than a year ago, during the summer of 2012, before Mario Draghi had uttered the "whatever it takes". I repeated our arguments for why a Private Sector Involvement ("PSI"), an ugly initialism synonymous with haircuts (losses) in the nominal value of bonds held by private sector investors, did not make sense in the case of Portugal. We argued, using a rough cost-benefit analysis, that the impact would be very small in terms of debt reduction and the consequences on European bond markets could be disproportionately negative. I was carefully going through the argument when I noticed, to my surprise, that a well-known Portuguese journalist was sitting at the end of the table. I learnt later that he was supposed to follow me in the speakers list. He had arrived earlier to the event and was invited by the investment banker to come in and listen to my delivery. Of course, part of the questions and discussions could easily be misinterpreted if taken out of context on the pages of a newspaper. At the time, I was a bit worried. I made a few calls to check if the journalist was a responsible one and would be aware of the sensitivity of the issues at stake. I was assured that he was. I warned the Ministry of Finance and waited anxiously for the next few days to see if the meeting was mentioned in the press. Only after the clean exit from the Troika program, more than six months later, did the journalist mention the meeting. In the editorial where he mentioned it, he was apologetic of our efforts to confront with analytical, logical arguments the skepticism of the investors gathered in front of us.

Portugal was scheduled to leave the adjustment program in April 2014. The country had less than six months to prove that it could finance itself independently of external official sources, replacing those with international investors. The cash that was accumulated by the State, mostly in the safe accounts of the Bank of Portugal, plus the contributions still to be received from the Troika would be enough to face expected State expenses in the meantime. But in previous years, new unexpected outlays had cropped up, in consequence of the economic and financial adjustment process Portugal was undergoing, due to either State-Owned Enterprises, bank recapitalization or bank unwinds. As I have discussed in previous chapters, the availability of cash and its expected uses was a constant theme of discussion with investors and a big focus for our team.

On the other hand, the domestic situation was still agitated. In August, the Constitutional Court had just decided that part of the measures taken to introduce more flexibility in public sector employment, agreed with the Troika as part of the adjustment program, were not constitutional. In addition, a new ruling on the proposed pension reform package was expected in next December. The government had opened a battle front with the Constitutional Court in the domestic press, questioning openly how the needed budgetary adjustment could be completed in light of the Court's regular negative rulings and constraining interpretations. These polemics were followed closely by investors that had taken, or were thinking of taking, big positions on Portuguese government bonds. Some investors were following the situation very closely. They made efforts to read the Portuguese newspapers, either using some interpretative approximations to the Portuguese language or chasing some Portuguese-speaking colleagues for quick translations. The theme had been a regular one in our conversations with investors during the entire 2013. The first Constitutional Court ruling of the year came in April and overruled a set of measures that had been included in the budget with the intention of containing the public sector wage bill.

In the twenty-first century, with our globalized information flows, it is difficult to keep domestic issues isolated from investors', the international press' or the rating agencies' attention. We had a sense that the government could be dramatizing the situation, putting some political pressure on the Constitutional Court as new decisions were expected. We decided that we should try to play our cards in anticipation and warn the government about the negative impact this strategy would have on our common effort to restore a solid market access in preparation for the approaching end of the program. Consequently, I requested a conversation with one of the advisors to the Prime Minister to warn him that an open confrontation with the Constitutional Court of the kind that was taking place could jeopardize market access. I explained our point during a Friday afternoon walk in the Prime Minister's residence gardens. It was a beautiful September afternoon and the Prime Minister was leaving earlier in his modest private car for a weekend with the family in the south of the country. I wandered the garden with his advisor, trying to explain my worries. I left with the impression that the level of reverberation that the controversy was having in the investor community came as a surprise to him. As expected, he was very focused on the domestic political battles. I hoped I made him see some glimpses of our day-to-day efforts in the outer galaxy of international markets, that I managed to express the need to consider our process when engaging in domestic politics and let go of some of the domestic skirmishes.

Following the exit from the program in April 2014, Portugal was facing a fork on the road leading to two very different outcomes: either a fully normalized access to the international bond market or a second program with some sort of continued support from the Troika. The first outcome, coined the "clean exit" in the press, involved continuous access to the markets to finance the still existing budget deficit and the regular bond repayments. The second outcome consisted in reality more than one: either a new full-fledged program of assistance like the Greek follow-on programs or a hybrid of Troika support and market access. This last outcome was being considered to deal with the scenario where Portugal would have some sort of market access but not robust enough to ensure ongoing regular access without some sort of backup support. The rationale for this alternative can be summarized in the following way: with a precautionary credit line available, investors would be more confident that in a scenario of lasting difficult market conditions and/or temporary investor loss of confidence, Portugal would still have access to backup funding and draw on the credit line in order to face its obligations vis-à-vis investors. These precautionary credit lines had played an important role during the financial crisis, reassuring investors in relation to Eastern Europe sovereigns.

It is very common to find situations in economic theory where there are multiple possible equilibria involving very different outcomes. I believe that during the fall of 2013 Portugal was facing two possible equilibria that would strongly influence the type of exit from the program available. Both involved some sort of feedback loop between investors' expectations and the experienced reality in the markets.

In the first equilibrium, which I will call the vicious one, investors do not expect Portugal to be able to normalize market access prior to the exit from the program. Or, using an even weaker condition, they expect that Portugal will not be able to restore a robust and durable market access and will, in some instances, still have to request extra assistance from its European partners. And if Portugal asked for extra assistance, investors believed that Europe could make its support conditional on investors taking losses on their bonds. As we have seen before, this is the specter of the Greek PSI that had been haunting the peripheral government bond crisis from its beginning. The moment in 2011, when the Europeans mentioned for the first time, that continuing support for Greece would implicate losses for investors in their holdings of Greek bonds, just confirming some fears that had been in the minds of investors since 2010. In addition, in 2013, confirming investors' anxiety, the IMF had produced a paper on sovereign restructuring. The possibility that any program extension could involve a haircut on private sector holdings meant that investors preferred to wait for market developments before acquiring important quantities of bonds either in the primary or in the secondary markets. Until market access was solid enough, this risk would keep hanging over the investors' willingness to build large positions of Portuguese government bonds in their portfolios.

In this case, investors prefer to wait and see what happens. They can safely wait for the end of the program and check if the risk materializes or not. This originates a vicious circle where the absence of market access becomes self-fulfilling. As investors wait, Portugal will not be able to access the primary market with new issues and then investors' expectations become confirmed by the reality in the markets.

In the second equilibrium, which I will call the virtuous one, investors build a strong conviction on the solidity of Portugal's market access. They expect that Portugal will not have to ask for any assistance in the near future. If not, they will not risk holding a large portfolio of bonds subject to the restructuring risk referred above. Without substantial restructuring risk, investors will be willing to take a large position in the bonds, probably as large as their degree of conviction allows. If they decide to wait, they may miss the train as the price of the bonds enters a period of appreciation.

In this case, the equilibrium becomes equally self-fulfilling. As investors are willing to increase their holdings of Portuguese bonds, it becomes easier for the sovereign to issue bonds using the primary markets and the prices tend to rise in the secondary markets as the demand for the bonds keeps increasing. The virtuous equilibrium becomes further and further confirmed by the reality in the markets. Investors' expectations are then confirmed by what they are seeing in the market. The ones that build the conviction earlier on reap the highest profits, since they get the bonds at prices at more depressed levels offered at an earlier stage in the process. As more and more investors get involved, attracted by the growing probability of a clean exit, the chances of a clean exit keep increasing, and so on, and so on, creating a clearer positive momentum in prices. The market for Portuguese government bonds will then enter positive dynamics that becomes self-sustained.

The big question is and was: can the debt manager through its strategy influence in some measure the type of equilibrium attainable? And in the affirmative case, how?

As you can easily deduce from the description of the two possible equilibria, it is crucial for investors to try to understand how other investors are thinking and what are others' expectations regarding the probabilities of a clean exit. Investors will try to infer if a positive consensus is building with enough strength to sustain positive price and volume dynamics in the markets. The extension of this support is important since no investor wants to be left by himself with bonds in a situation where the demand for the bonds disappears. At the time, investors were evaluating if there was a critical mass of other investors to sustain the clean exit from the program without the need for further official support. It is like the game of musical chairs. The music stops and there is nothing the investor can do, just take losses in bonds no one wants to buy. It might be too late to sell out of the accumulated bond position before a decision about further official support involving an eventual haircut is taken.

Investors can try to learn about other investors' beliefs, by exchanging ideas and convictions with others when attending presentations, by reading what is being written in the financial press and in the wires or, most crucially, by observing market action and getting market color from their dealers, the investment banks.

I believe that, at this point, the capital of trust and credibility of the debt manager plays an important role as well. He should show confidence that he has developed a strategy that will allow him to achieve the desired outcome. Of course, we are speaking here about realistic expectations, not artificial ones. Credibility is an important asset for a debt manager.

During the IMF meetings of October 2014, we were invited for lunch by the Portuguese Ambassador to Washington and by the governor of the Bank of Portugal. In addition to the governor some other Bank of Portugal senior staff were attending. The governor asked me about the strategy we had thought in view of obtaining a clean exit. I outlined our plans in broad terms, as the specifics would still be part of future conversations with the Minister of Finance. One of the Bank of Portugal directors reacted with some surprise at how confidently we stated our plans. He asked why we thought the market conditions would be there, allowing us to achieve our targets. He followed up on his worries regarding our bullishness and asked us for our plan B. I told him there was no plan B (whatever plan B might exist was outside our remit anyway). I mentioned that when you are following a narrow path in a steep gorge over a rushing and freezing river you just look ahead and move on. If you think too much about your plan B, a freezing swim might become your reality very soon. I am not sure if he was very appeased by my reply.

In our quest to achieve a positive market dynamic that would support a virtuous equilibrium, we were thinking about which transactions to bring to the market in the next few months. We were very aware that these transactions would be very closely scrutinized by investors in their evaluation of Portugal's odds of a clean market exit from the program. In that sense, the way we were going to communicate with the outside world in the next few months would be more important than ever. The perception investors would build on the back of our next moves was going to be crucial to build their conviction regarding the strength of Portugal's position in the markets. We needed to use the series of transactions we were planning to execute as an engine to create enough of a forward thrust and to engage more and more investors in our bonds, helping to generate the needed critical mass.

So, similar to our choice in 2012, when we had to come out with a one year ahead financing plan to present to the Troika, and influenced by the good memories of this initial transaction, we proposed to the Ministry of Finance a bond exchange. The rationale was, similar to 2012, to prepare for the issuance of bonds we were planning for the start of the year 2014. We were looking to alleviate the financial needs for the next two years and make investors comfortable with the feasibility of our financing plans in the near term. The idea was to offer investors the possibility to exchange bonds that were coming close to being repaid, in 2014 and 2015, for longer bonds. If the transaction was successful, the amount of bond repayments in the near future would decrease and extend to longer dates. Then, the next two years would be easier to manage and pressure would be taken out from the volume needed from the market around the end of the Troika's program. We expected this transaction to put us in a position where we would become a more independent issuer, more relaxed and less constrained by market timing—to show to the investor community that the Debt Management Office was free to decide when and how much to issue without being conditioned by immediate needs (in this case the consequences of the end of the program). It is never good to look in despair for cash when you are looking to issue bonds and always better to look in control and unconcerned by specific circumstances and current market conditions.

The transaction would have to be prepared very carefully. It was going to be the first of what we expected to be a series of transactions that would take us to a comfortable position ahead of the end of the program. We were aiming to impress the market with the transaction in terms of investor participation. It was important not to create too high a level of expectation to start with but to present it almost as a natural housekeeping transaction in preparation for the crucial start of the year that was to follow. Keep it low profile so that, if we were successful and surpassed a moderate level of expectations, the transaction could help us in the process of building a positive momentum ahead of what we expected to be a powerful start of the year 2014 in terms of issuance.

When preparing for this transaction, we were fortunate to be able to revisit the 2015 maturity bond that had already been the object of our 2012 exchange. We had a good idea where a good chunk of the bonds were, and this made it easier when trying to understand the willingness of certain investors to participate in a transaction of this kind. The 2012 exchange had involved €3.75 billion in bonds, which were mostly sitting in the bond portfolios of domestic investors (the original issue had mostly been sold domestically). We had already signaled that a transaction of this kind could be in the horizon but we tended to downplay its importance each time we talked about it. Preparing for the transaction, we had an idea where the market expected participation to be. In addition, inferring from the conversations we had, including with our primary dealers, we expected to be able to execute a transaction surpassing those expectations. Of course, all this is always far from certain and you always take a fair amount of risk up to the day when the transaction takes place.

On the day, you wake up without knowing if all your calculations make sense and if, in spite of all the planning, you do not have a transaction flop ahead of you. At least, in the case of the exchanges, you are limited to the short time (one hour generally) during which the auction and the reverse auction take place. During that time you invite investors to participate in a reverse auction for the bonds you are offering to buy so that they are replaced by the bonds you are offering to sell. Both processes take place simultaneously in the Bloomberg auction system which is in front of all participants. The primary dealers insert the parallel requests for both selling and buying in the system at the relative prices at which different investors are willing to participate. Then you decide the cutoff price considering that all investors that show willingness to offer a relative price that is higher or equal to the cutoff will have their bonds exchanged. As is usual in this type of transactions, we would all gather in the dealing room of the Debt Management Office, at the start of the process, behind Rita, responsible for the trading department, and await anxiously for developments as the different orders from the primary dealers hit the screens. We see the orders, with their sizes and relative prices, accumulate in the screen, and as the clock ticks, we understand if the transaction is going to be successful or not. In the case of this specific transaction, as the orders accumulated it was pretty clear that participation was not only overshooting what we believed to be investors' expectations but also our own. It became clear that the transaction was going to be a big success.

We had exchanged close to one-third of the bond that ended its life in October 2015 (close to €4 billion), which we believed was more than what the investors were expecting for the full transaction size. And, in addition, we had relieved part of the 2014 redemptions, close to €837 million of the bond which ended its life in June 2014 and €1.7 billion of the bond with maturity in October 2014. We would still need to issue close to €2.5 billion less in 2014 to cover for the year's financing needs. But We were saving a bond issuance during the year, alleviating our short-term situation. Furthermore, investors had preferred to extend their commitment to Portuguese government bonds. Close to €4 billion in holdings had been exchanged into the June 2018 bond while €2.675 billion was exchanged into the October 2017 bond. This was an additional data point emphasizing the increased confidence of investors on the Portuguese market resilience following the end of the adjustment program.

Following the transaction, it was important to communicate to the press how successful the transaction was, in terms of both the size and the fact that the longer maturities were favored, demonstrating investor trust in Portugal. Additionally, there was a message of continuity and consistency in our part as we kept working to smoothen the redemption profile and alleviate short-term financing needs. We kept working to be in control of the situation, and following this transaction we improved our position and autonomy.

It was crucial now to prepare for the next step and to indicate the succession of steps we were intending to take to cross the bridge into sturdy market access. We knew January could provide us with good market conditions to issue into, given the positive momentum. In addition, in January, asset managers normally are shopping for bonds as they allocate and adjust their portfolios as they receive more cash. We were anticipating a strong 2014 opening for issuance in general. So, we had to start managing expectations taking this into consideration. We had to prepare and focus investors toward what we were planning to do, to solidify their conviction that Portugal would not need a second support package from its European partners. If we pre-announced a path and then we hit every milestone with success, we believed we would definitely be out of the woods.

We packed our bags and went to London again to visit the financial press and the wires. We were going to brag about the transaction we had just executed but also to convey a message of optimism for the start of the year and a strong outlook for issuance in January and February. We commuted from office to office across London, consistently delivering our message with the unwavering support of our communications advisory company. One of the main financial newspapers published an article that mentioned our visit and with subtle English irony expressed some doubts in relation to our confidence in our plans.

They were not the only ones; some of the members of the Portuguese government were skeptical at the time. In the meantime, another decision from the Constitutional Court was announced: it sent the pension reform proposed by the government back to the drawing board. Surprisingly (or not) the market did not react negatively. We saw it as a good omen, a sign that the positive current that was being created was starting to run deep. But in the political trenches of government, there was still a strong emphasis on the ongoing confrontation with the Constitutional Court. Every defeat was deeply felt, as a confirmation of how difficult it was to change the country and to solve in a durable way the structural problems of the

Portuguese state. When we mentioned our intention to request for authorization to issue bonds as the market re-opened in January and supported this with our optimistic market views, we had to face the doubts raised by the Ministry of Finance. These officials did not see why the Portuguese government bonds would start trading in appreciation mode following what happened in December, that is, the latest negative Constitutional Court decision. They said something like: "for sure, there had been no reaction to the Constitutional Court decision because in December the market was not liquid enough; the market was dormant, but in January, investors would understand the negative impact of this ruling for the continuation of the state reform process." Their expectation was, opposite to ours, that the market conditions for Portuguese government bonds would worsen at the start of the year, making it difficult to issue and build a virtuous momentum. Whatever their beliefs, we were confirmed that in case of a virtuous re-opening in January, we would be duly authorized to take advantage of the circumstances.

As we had predicted, the market opened strongly for Portuguese government bonds in January. As agreed in December, we came to the Ministry of Finance with our proposal and a positive recommendation on the part of our primary dealers. We were authorized to go ahead with some changes to our proposal. There was some discussion regarding the choice of bond to tap (we were going to use an existing bond and increase its size instead of issuing a new bond). We defended a longer maturity could make sense to prove more decisively how supportive investors were. This, in our view, could accelerate the process and reinforce expectations of a clean exit from the program. The Ministry defended that if we believed that we would be able to issue more than once, it would make sense to start with shorter maturities for reasons of cost. At the start of a series of issuances, when the yields are higher, it will cost more to issue and it would make sense, then, to commit to this higher cost for less time by issuing a shorter maturity bond. Then, as the virtuous cycle reinforced a positive performance, we could issue longer bonds at a lower yield. It made sense and in hindsight the Minister of Finance took the right decision. In conclusion, we moved ahead by tapping a bond that would mature in June 2019.

We woke up on 9 January with some strong indications from the previous day but, as usual, with still a lot of uncertainty in the air. I woke up very calm, knowing that each step during the day, up to the pricing of the bond after lunch, would be crucial. I was in execution mode. A lot of the adrenaline of this job would concentrate on that day. And it would be possible that the day would only end at dinner time in the TV channel newscast studio. I would not be thinking about the next step, but focusing on each moment fully, to avoid any mistake. We knew that every decision could have consequences on interest costs for the State for years to come. Spotless execution demanded a full presence at each step in the transaction execution.

We had prepared to move early in the month as we wanted to pick the first buying flows from investors. We picked a period with very low competing supply of bonds by similar issuers. At 7.30 AM we had our call with the banks that had been picked to help us attract investors to the bond. As usual, we had to confirm if we still felt confident to move ahead with the transaction in light of the investors' feedback provided by the banks. This was followed by the decision about where the pricing discussion should start. If the first price indication starts from a lower level, it may allow us to attract investors and build momentum so that we can adjust prices later. The momentum in these transactions is very important as a good vibe around the transaction tends to attract more interest and may build the perception that the bonds will perform well after issuance, in the secondary market. On the negative side, it tends to attract more opportunistic buyers that just want to buy for the quick profit. This drawback can be mitigated when deciding on the investors to attribute bonds to, after the transaction is closed for new orders. A strong positive momentum can facilitate a shorter transaction, allowing the issuer to close the books to new orders faster. Starting with a higher price indication decreases the margin of maneuver for adjustments in price later on and can cause orders for the bond to build in a slower fashion; it may make for less dynamic execution days.

Following the meeting, at 8 AM, we started getting indications of interest on the part of investors at the initial price indication, called "price talk." Officially, the "books" opened at 9.15 AM, meaning that the banks could start confirming the orders for the bonds and we could all see them in the shared IT system. We did not need to gather around a computer as we all had access to the system from our computers and could see the orders coming in and the "book" building up. Each order is a line indicating the investor name, the desired amount and if there is any condition linked to the order (for instance, maximum price). Orders can be altered at any point until the "books" close. At 9: 15 we had €5 billion of orders. At that point we had not indicated what would be the size of the transaction; we only said it was going to be big enough, a benchmark size, so that investors expect the bond to be liquid in the secondary market when it starts trading. We were intending to issue more than €2.5 billion, hopefully, to guarantee the "benchmark size." By 10: 45 we had €11 billion of orders. We had increased the price already once. We decided to increase it one more time, announce a size of €3.25 billion and close the "book," asking the banks to confirm the orders with their clients.

We were happy with the investor composition. It showed a diversity of investor types coming from diverse geographies; 280 investors had shown interest in the transaction. There was a good share of global asset managers, more than 60%, and 7.2% of pension funds and insurance companies, which though not being a lot, showed some interest from traditionally more conservative and long-term investors. We still had more than 15% of the hedge funds, indicating that we were still in the process of normalizing market access but also that there was an expectation of price appreciation. At this point in the day, we still had a lot of work to do: deciding with the banks how many bonds to give to each investor. We had more than €11 billion of orders and we only intended to increase the existing bond by €3.25 billion. Figure out doing this for 280 investors!

In the afternoon, after pricing the transaction, we had to prepare the press release with the banks. Usually, in the afternoon we also received some calls from journalists, domestic and foreign. That afternoon we received one that made us all particularly proud. It was from the financial newspaper that had expressed some doubts regarding our plans after our last visit to London. The markets editor wanted to congratulate us and confirmed that we looked too optimistic when we visited. He mentioned that our visit had been discussed at the editorial board and that skepticism was consensual. He recognized that we had been right and that what we predicted had happened. So, now, they wanted to ask us what our plans were for the near future and how we were expecting the markets for Portuguese bonds to evolve from here. We mentioned that we expected the market to react very positively to our transaction and the prices of our bonds to continue to rise. Therefore, we should be coming back to the markets to issue bonds in the very near future and probably with a longer maturity. It will then be obvious that we will be on our way to fully re-access the markets in the same way as we used to do before the crisis. We will be on our way to achieving a clear and clean exit from the adjustment program! Next day, the article mentioning our transaction in the financial newspaper was celebratory and did not include the pinch of irony of previous pieces about the Portuguese process for regaining bond market access.

On 11 February we were back in the market, re-opening a bond that would mature in 2024, increasing it by €3 billion. We closed the books at 10.30 AM counting €9.8 billion of orders. In this transaction, hedge funds only represented 4% of the bonds allocated to investors. Investors from Scandinavia and Benelux, traditionally more conservative geographies, represented 25% of the bonds sold.

This follow-on transaction showed we could sell bonds from longer maturities. Since our previous transaction the yield on our ten-year bonds (interest paid) had come from 6.1% to just below 5%, an amazing performance that vindicated the Ministry of Finance's strategic option of issuing shorter maturities first.

In addition, we were building a sizeable cash buffer for Portugal that would allow us to live comfortably through the year, and we were only in February. We did not need to issue any more to achieve the cash needed for a clean exit from the program. We obviously advertised this cash buffer. This became a political issue when in the parliament we were questioned about the cost involved in having this amount of cash accumulated in the bank accounts, mostly with the bank of Portugal, that was offering interest rates on the deposits that were close to zero.

The positive momentum in our government bond market was now firmly established. The clean exit that some viewed with skepticism only one month ago was now, quickly, becoming consensual. Investors that were latecomers in our market were now looking to buy to take advantage of some of the remaining potential for convergence with core government bonds. The case of Ireland came to their minds, and more and more investors saw the possibility of achieving still more price appreciation.

We were now in full virtuous cycle!

A few months later, when passing through New York, we met an investor that we suspected had been a strong buyer of our bonds during the previous November. He confirmed that had been the case. We inquired about his motivation. He told us that there were two main triggers: firstly, when he visited Portugal (he had been part of the group to which I had presented in the hotel when a journalist was present), he built the conviction that the Constitutional Court was not an insurmountable barrier for the Portuguese adjustment process and that it was only playing a natural checks and balances role; secondly, when he came through London and spoke with dealers, he understood they were stocking inventories of

Portuguese government bonds. As the banks speak to everyone, if they were stocking the bonds, it meant they were expecting demand, so other investors must have been positive on our projects too. He probably wanted to be in pole position to take advantage of the expected price move and so decided to make the case to his investment committee. I am sure in February he was very happy with his decision.

References

1. António Garcia Pascual. "More Funding and Debt Relief Needed." Barclays Economics Research, (October 2013).
2. International Monetary Fund. "Portugal, Eighth and Ninth Review." (November 2013).
3. IGCP. "Notes on Recent Macro Developments." (January 21, 2014).
4. IGCP. "EUR 3.25 Bn OT Syndicated Tap due 14 June 2019." Press Release. (January 9, 2014).
5. IGCP. "€3.0 Billion OT Syndicated Reopening due 15 February 2024." Press Release. (February 11, 2014).
6. European Stability Mechanism. "Guideline on Precautionary Financial Assistance." (October 2012).

CHAPTER 8

Success

Abstract This chapter describes the final steps taken to ensure full bond market access. Portugal organized the first Portuguese auction process for medium to long term bonds since requesting the Troika's assistance. In May 2014, Portugal exited the Troika program with no need for further assistance. It did not ask for the last disbursement from the Troika. Market conditions for Portuguese bonds continued to improve. A USD transaction was executed that helped to reinforce Portugal's cash buffer. Our description of the Portuguese economic adjustment with a strong contribution from exports became widespread. We managed to attract several different investors to our markets. They have sustained us throughout. I discuss what could have been the alternative if Portugal would have had to request continued support from Europe. This alternative would have been costlier for the Portuguese population and put the nascent economic recovery at risk. The Portuguese public opinion was conscious of the value of market access and it became consensual across party lines. It had been crucial to gain access to a diversified investor base and maintain a constant and credible dialogue with investors both directly and through the press. It was key to keep actions predictable when dealing with investors in the markets.

Keywords Precautionary line • Bond auctions • Portugal clean exit • Economic adjustment • Bond market access • Sovereign credibility

J. M. Rato, *The European Debt Crisis*,
https://doi.org/10.1007/978-3-030-61174-3_8

Following the February bond issuance, we were in a very comfortable position to face the State's financing needs for 2014. We had proved we had access to the bond market in size. The financing needs for 2014 were estimated to be close to €30 billion. We had started the year with €15 billion in deposits and were still expecting to receive €5 billion from the final tranches of the Troika loans. In the first two months of the year we had issued more than €6 billion in bonds. So we were just short of €4 billion for the year and there were ten months to go. In addition, the conditions in the secondary market were just getting better and better. Ten-year yields on Portuguese government bonds had come from close to 6% at the end of 2013 to a yield of 5.11% when we issued a ten-year bond in February. As you may remember from Chap. 6, Ireland had issued at 4.11% at the start of 2013, setting them up for an exit from their Troika program. We had some catching up to do, but by May Portugal's ten-year yield was lower than 4%. The markets were demonstrating every day by trading at lower levels of yields that we had investors' support. We were successfully embarking on a positive, self-reinforcing, momentum that would take us out of the Troika program without the need to negotiate further assistance. The signs of support from investors could not be clearer, as the prices of bonds were steadily moving up in response to the transactions that we had executed at the start of the year. The secondary market conditions were more stable and the volumes traded had shot up since January. Before January most of the volumes traded were over the counter (one on one between primary dealers and investors or other primary dealers). Since then, we were seeing a resurgence of trading in platforms. This meant that traders and investors were more comfortable in executing their orders using machines instead of calling banks, indicating that the market was normalizing.

As you may remember from a previous discussion, Portugal's access to the bond markets before the crisis consisted of issuing new bonds through syndication and subsequently tapping those bonds using a regular auction calendar. And we had been telling investors, the press and the rating agencies, we were looking to restore the same type of market access that we had before the crisis. As a next step, we needed to work toward restoring regular auctions for the bonds with maturity up to ten years. The Troika program was scheduled to end on 17 May 2014, so we had to move fast as, by that date, everything would have to be in place for scheduled bond auctions. To achieve this in such a short time would not be an easy task. The positive dynamics created by our start of the year transactions was helping.

But it was still a challenge. To participate in auctions, investors have to be comfortable that the price at which they take the bonds in the auction is close to where the bonds are trading in the secondary market. If the price moves against them following the auction they will face losses. As the auction is a much less controlled environment than selling bonds through a syndication process, it can generate price discontinuities in the secondary market. On the other hand, if the prices are very volatile in the secondary markets it becomes difficult for investors to accept to commit to a given price in the auction. So, for an issuer to be able to use auctions, the underlying price volatility of bonds has to be moderated and the auction process itself has to result from prices that are close to secondary market prices.

The strategic behavior of primary dealers participating in the auction can generate price distortions. They have incentives to behave strategically because they use auction participation to get a good ranking. And a good ranking will enable them to participate in the more profitable syndicated issues. This may lead them to bond overbidding in the auction, creating prices that are artificially high when compared with the secondary market. As strategic behavior can generate high price swings, we had to make sure this type of strategic behavior was discouraged. If not, the auctions can disturb the stability of the secondary market prices and this lack of stability will discourage final investors to participate in the auctions.

When we prepared for the first auction, we had the very helpful assistance of the Portuguese Ambassador in the UK. To discuss the rules of engagement in the auctions, we gathered the representatives of the different primary dealers at the Portuguese embassy in London. We met at a very grand room in the embassy, which is located in Belgravia. It has a tapestry representing Catarina de Bragança, the Portuguese wife of Charles II. The Ambassador set up the mood for the meeting with an institutional presentation with references to this queen that contributed to the solidification of the relations between Portugal and England. Following the Ambassador's presentation, I set up the rules for primary dealers' participation in auctions, stressing the importance of good behavior and the penalties to be implemented for those breaking the rules. The introduction of auctions had to be a success. If it resulted in the perception that we were moving too fast and the market for Portuguese bonds was still unprepared, the consequences could be dire. We were risking the reversion of the positive momentum in the bond market. In addition, we risked being marked by rating agencies and the Troika as being unable to restore full market access and jeopardize our efforts. To try to mitigate this downside, it was decided to use a pricing system in the auction, single price, where the sovereign took relatively more risk than in other price mechanisms. The stakes were too high to go for other auction methodologies where investors would be asked to take up a bigger share of the risk.

On 23 April, we were able to auction the ten-year bond that was sold in February, at 3.59%, more than 1 percentage point lower than the yield that we had paid the market at issuance. As expected, the size placed in the auction was almost ten times lower than what we had been able to place through syndication. In addition, we survived the process and could convince the market that we were able to execute auctions in a regular fashion. We would come back to tap the same bonds using an auction on 11 June at a yield of 3.28%. At that point, we had the same type of market access that we had before the crisis and achieved what the Boston asset manager had predicted for us back in January 2013, when he had made an analogy with Mexico in the 1990s.

As had been the case since 2012, Portugal was playing catch up with Ireland. By the end of 2013, Ireland had built a cash buffer that covered its financing needs for 12–15 months.[1] They had issued a ten-year bond in January 2014 at 3.54%. Portugal yields caught up to those levels in April, very swiftly, sustained by the positive effect created by the two bonds issued at the beginning of the year. It was also in 2014 that Ireland managed to re-establish regular auctions, at least once a quarter, using the single price mechanism. Irish bond yields also experienced a decline, and according to the Irish DMO: "2014 was deemed to be the year in which full market access was restored." Our timing ended up by being not so different from the Irish one. Ireland had left its adjustment program in December 2013.

Greece played the role of the counterfactual. During 2014, Greek ten-year yields had been coming down, but by February they were still at 7%, whereas the minimum was reached in July at a level close to 6%. At these yields it was very difficult to issue bonds. The investors involved in Greek bonds were still mostly from the distressed hedge fund community. Greece was still at the start of the investor relay race described in Chap. 4, at the same stage we had been in 2012. They had, in the meantime, benefitted from a haircut, which reduced their bond redemptions in the short term.

[1] As described in the Irish experience in "Assessing sovereign markets – the recent experiences of Ireland, Portugal, Spain and Cyprus".

By the end of April, Portugal was in a comfortable position. At the time, a senior government official told the *Financial Times*: "The great thing is to have a choice (between a clean exit and a credit line). Eight months to a year ago, not many people saw that as likely."[2] On 4 May the government announced that it was exiting the program without a precautionary credit line. In addition, Portugal decided not to draw on the last scheduled disbursement from the Troika, an amount approximating €3 billion.

To make sure that there was enough of a cash buffer, the Treasury and Debt Management Office for Portugal ("IGCP") embarked on another transaction: issuing in USD. The transaction would allow us to build up a stronger cash buffer and diversify the instruments available to the sovereign. It was executed in July and contributed $4.5 billion or the equivalent to €3.3 billion, making up for the government's decision not to take up the last Troika tranche.

As we have discussed briefly in Chap. 2, part of our funding plans included the re-activation of retail products. These savings products had been sacrificed during the period preceding the government call for external assistance. The interest offered on the savings certificates had been reduced unilaterally, making them less interesting in comparison with bank term deposits. This decision eroded the trust that existed between the State and the retail investors. These were products that had been sold since the 1960s, using the post office network, to moms and pops. The average investments were low. Savings certificates had represented 15% of Portuguese government debt in 2008, but only represented 7% in 2011. Very early on, with the strong support from the Minister of Finance and António Borges, and in the face of strong lobbying by the banks, we managed to increase the rate that was offered for these products. During 2013, they already contributed €1.1 billion of net funding. But for 2014, we were more ambitious, as we were launching a new type of instrument for retail investors that we believed would be very successful. It was a dated savings certificate with a fixed maturity, contrary to the existing ones, that were redeemable at all times following an initial period, but had no fixed maturity. This new instrument would offer an increasing coupon, providing an incentive for investors to keep the certificate until its final maturity date. It included a fancy feature: at maturity it offered an extra income

[2] "Portugal to exit €78bn bailout without emergency backstop", *Financial Times*, April 30, 2014.

linked to the Portuguese economic growth during the period (GDP linked). We were expecting retail products to contribute €3 billion during 2014. This increase in retail products take down, produced a side benefit: it showed external investors that domestic investors had confidence in the Portuguese adjustment and were willing to take on some risk too. They understood that these products were very widely distributed through the Portuguese population.

The succession of bond transactions and the ramping up of retail products' issuance allowed Portugal to fully re-establish market access and to approach the following year with a comfortable cash buffer. The alternative would have been to seek a precautionary credit line from our European Union partners. But as the Prime Minister was quoted saying to the *Financial Times* in April, it was not clear what a credit line would entail: "the prime minister said the disadvantage of seeking an ESM [European Stability Mechanism] credit line was that such a safety net had never been negotiated before, making it unclear what conditions would be attached to it." Would Portugal have to subscribe to a set of conditions that, in practice, were very similar to a program, including more austerity measures? What about investors' fears that a haircut could be attached to any further assistance? This looked probable as our European partners would have to sell this new type of support to their domestic audiences and obtain the approval of their parliaments. And, at the time, there was a big resistance on the part of the public opinion of some European countries for providing more backing to the European periphery.

I had been invited by the Minister of Economy to join him in a visit to one of the countries in Northern Europe. The visit included a meeting followed by a dinner with a very important investor. When I joined the travelling team, which included the Portuguese Ambassador with whom I had maintained an active dialogue during the previous year, they had already met with the country's government. They had been conveyed a clear advice: we should work to achieve a clean exit from the program without the need for any further support. Any type of support would be very difficult to approve domestically, at least without attaching to it tough conditions. Their parliament was not very open to approve further support without some extra austerity measures.

This visit occurred toward the end of 2013. At the beginning of 2014, we were on a roadshow in another Northern European country and were invited to present our plans for regaining market access at the Ministry of Finance. Following a presentation to higher officials in the Ministry, they invited us for lunch. During lunch, they emphasized how much they admired our work and what we had already achieved but ... They had a junior coalition party in government that would resist conceding Portugal any further support. They had elections coming in the next year and would be in a difficult position if they were perceived as planning to put more of their taxpayers' money at risk in Southern Europe. The message was clear and consistent with what our Prime Minister told the *Financial Times* in April. The timing was not good to request further support from our European partners. The public opinion in Central and Northern Europe was exhausted with the peripheral crisis. This was to become clear during 2015 in Greece.

You may remember that in Chap. 2 we identified three challenges we were facing in 2012: to re-establish a credible and verifiable narrative for the Portuguese sovereign as a basis for our regular communication with investors, the press, rating agencies and primary dealers; to rebuild a diversified investor base; and to deal with the legacy issues concerning the region of Madeira and the state-owned enterprises.

The latter one had given us a lot of work, mainly during the renegotiation of the swaps contracts that the public sector companies had contracted with investment banks and were now a very high liability for those companies. This piece of work included two long sessions in the parliament to explain what we were doing. It demanded a very meticulous process management so that we could keep the negotiation team completely segregated from the rest of the IGCP. The rest of the institution had to keep a regular working contact with the investment banks. These were a very important conduit in the process of re-establishing market access for our bonds. As we have seen, it was crucial that the renegotiations did not contaminate our relationships with primary dealers and jeopardize our reputation in the market. So, the team renegotiating the swaps portfolio had to be hermetically isolated from the rest of the institution. In addition, the issue became very political, which made confidentiality difficult to maintain.

In addition, some creditors were still trying to use any far-fetched argument available to activate an early redemption clause for the bonds and loans from Portuguese public sector companies that they owned. This took, also, a substantial part of our time and attention. I could write another book on these two topics. For what concerns us here, we had to make sure there was no negative reputational impact, that we were not jeopardizing important relationships or contributing to frightening press headlines raising the fear of unknown liabilities to the State. Investors worried that the impact of these issues could prove too much for the State to handle, that they could put our efforts at re-establishing market access at risk. We had frequent questions on those topics in roadshows.

The description of the Portuguese economic and financial adjustment process and of the Portuguese economy became slowly widespread. Portugal's exporting structure and performance became well known. Even the most reluctant journalist in the economic press came to accept the facts. It helped that our presentations rested on data. As we emphasized in Chap. 3, the export story played a very important role. And I really believed that it changed the external image of Portugal and that it changed the way the press referred to Portugal. We started to present Portugal as a different country from the then dominant stereotypes—a country with a more modern productive structure, integrated higher up in the global value chains, not dependent on cheap unskilled labor and natural resources, with stronger institutions. It was very different from the backward image the country had before. As I mentioned in Chap. 3, at the end of the process, investors when comparing Portugal with Greece would flag that Portugal had a higher exporting capacity and stronger institutions. This was not what investors believed at the beginning of the process. Portugal's image in the world continued to improve following 2014. But I believe the change started there, at that moment in time when, because of the sad circumstances, the world was paying attention to our country. Our story was interesting in the context of the European crisis. At the start of the process, investors tended to see us as closer to the Greek situation than to the Irish. Following two years of constant travelling and presentations, the perception changed. And I will always remember the combative posture of Cristina in fighting for our points. Then, of course, the facts proved that the reality was developing in a consistent manner with what we were saying. Our credibility rested on that. We were always very much aware that if we became disconnected from what the data were telling us we would jeopardize our position vis-à-vis investors, the press and the rating agencies. We were rebuilding trust. And as we have seen in Chap. 6, the path we followed was not a straight line; sometimes we fell, had to stand up again and fight on.

Greece's yields had been coming down and the situation there had been stabilizing, but the yields were still too high for them to access the market. One of the main obstacles they were facing was the lack of an investor base, both in number and diversification. Remember that we had close to 300 investors participating in our syndicated issues. And, in addition, we were able to involve multiple types of investors coming from different geographies. We aimed to attract to our market investors with different objectives, needing our bonds for different reasons. This diversity allows for a deeper market. As in a more diversified ecosystem there is more action, a more diverse investor base sustains more transactions in the secondary market. And, at issuance, if a specific geography and investor type is conditioned due to external circumstances, others can come in. We always looked at this effort as work in progress. We were always searching for the next frontier. We were already meeting with Japanese investors even if we knew it was probably too soon for them to get involved in our bonds. We continued to insist in Germany, not always with a lot of success. We were trying to visit the Middle East even if local investors did not look very receptive. The relay race continued and a deep market was crucial for price stability. There is no doubt that the level of involvement by investors generated in 2014 allowed us to move faster into auctions. Reality in the markets became too strong for a very skeptical ESM and other European institutions: I believe they were, among our stakeholders, the last ones to believe we were going to be successful in restoring market access. But we had our fingers in the markets' pulse, and we could see more and more investors coming in, wanting to benefit from what was looking like Portugal's success story. Even the crisis affecting one of the big domestic banks during the summer did not manage to derail the positive momentum.

As we have seen, to get investors on our side, to count with their support, it was also crucial to manage other stakeholders: the press and the rating agencies. Regarding the former, we had the precious collaboration of one of the top communications advisory firms in the world that helped us navigate the media. This was not enough: we had to always make sure we were delivering a consistent message. We were very tragic in our interactions with the press: we thought any mistake could prove fatal. Sometimes we suffered, sometimes we did not sleep, but we managed to keep attention switched on and never slack, remembering that there is no such thing as an off-the-record conversation. I will always remember the story one of our bankers told us. He received a call from a local journalist asking him for a secret report and assured him no one would know that he was the source. He replied sincerely that he was a Catholic and for that reason, in his case, there was always someone important that knew. I tried to make sure that we implemented that principle at the IGCP: everything we produced could be leaked and anything we told journalists could be misinterpreted and badly reproduced. So, we should be able to defend, rationalize and fit in the big picture everything we wrote and said.

Regarding the rating agencies, we were not as successful. We repeated the same conversations over and over again. Sometimes we had the sensation we were speaking to a wall. It was clear that unless they started to see our public debt decreasing in a sustainable way, they would remain skeptical and consequently immobile. We had the sensation that the role of keeping a close relationship with the rating agencies was more aimed at managing the downside. They could write something that could really derail our efforts. This was the case when one rating agency wanted to write that Portugal's reforms could be reversed, without having any evidence. We had to stay on top of what they were writing to make sure that negative stereotypes did not spill into their regular reports. Those were very frustrating relationships. I believe they could have moved positively earlier and they could have been slower in pacing the downgrades, mostly in 2012.

It is clear that what was commonly called the clean exit from the Troika program allowed Portugal to avoid another round of conditionality. A precautionary credit line or a full program would have come with more conditions: austerity measures to give comfort to voters of the countries that were providing the support. Part of these conditions would have been politically motivated: to show that you are tough with debtors, and even tougher with debtors that need your help repeatedly. There is a demonstrative dimension in these packages. Just consider the arm wrangling with Greece in 2015 and the primary surplus that was demanded from the Greek government on that occasion: 3.5%. This was the surplus in their public accounts when you do not account for the interest payments on the public debt. Did this make sense given that the Greek gross domestic product was contracting in 2015 again after it had done so for six of the previous seven years?

I believe the Portuguese public opinion understood that an extra round of measures dictated by external creditors could be noxious for the nascent recovery that was just showing its first signs. They understood that investors would not be keen on the same package of measures as a new program would demand. Investors did not have the same objective function as the politicians. They have to sell more sovereign support to their constituencies. Bond investors would like to see on the part of the authorities a continuation of discipline but in a way that would not damage the expected economic recovery. They supported reforms that brought higher efficiency to the economy but were expecting time to be given for the reforms that were already in place to produce results. Investors generally invest in highly indebted countries when they expect those to grow out of debt. If they expect an economy to fall into a negative contractionary spiral, they will tend not to invest. They generally benefit from higher returns in countries that enter a period of public debt reduction, as long as not driven by inflation or currency depreciation. As Portugal could not reduce debt by inflating or depreciating the currency and did not depend on itself to reduce it via debt repression (keeping interest rates artificially low), the country had to mainly grow out of its debt problem. Investors are professionals and have followed a lot of similar situations in the past.

As we have seen in Chap. 2, the social situation reached a trough in Portugal in 2013. Since then, unemployment started to drop as jobs started to be created again in the economy, firstly mostly low-paid jobs and in tourism, then it generalized to the rest of the economy. Youth unemployment started to decrease and emigration slowed. The period of panic, when the population was always uncertain about which new austerity measures would be implemented and who would be impacted, pensioners, public servants or income tax payers, had passed. Public opinion was keen on leaving the Troika program behind. Access to the markets was the available alternative and was embraced by a large chunk of the population. To maintain a healthy relationship with investors became valued by a large part of the electorate. The fact that, even following a change in government, with a left-wing coalition in power, success came to be measured based on yield compression, market support and rating agencies' upgrades is demonstrative. The adjustment period created in the public opinion the perception that investors in Portuguese bonds were important to maintain the Troika at bay and make their life better. It was a relief not to have to constantly negotiate new policies with creditors using a very convoluted mechanism that only tended to increase uncertainty. Market demands were perceived to be more straightforward and simpler to understand.

Market conditions in Portugal following the exit from the program maintained a certain stability even in the presence of the financial stress that affected one of the big commercial banks. The change in government and the transfer of NovoBanco Bonds in a manner that looked discretionary to investors delayed the compression in yields. The bond transfer had the most relevant impact, as some investors were not expecting this action—exactly the type of things the previous government looked to avoid: surprising investors with negative news. But when it became clear that the new government would proceed on the path of fiscal discipline, the economy would keep growing moderately and therefore debt reduction would proceed at a good pace, yields continued to tighten.

In the meantime, the IGCP received two international prizes relative to its actions in 2014 that left us very proud. These prizes had the equivalent significance of Oscars for issuers and for specific transactions. The IGCP was considered the sovereign issuer of the year for the International Financing Review ("IFR"), which was a prize that Portugal had never received before and is normally attributed to much bigger sovereign issuers. When attributing the prize, the IFR explained: "from moving inexorably up the maturity curve, through reinstating its auction programme, to exiting the EU/IMF bailout, Portugal made strides in returning to funding normality in 2014. It rode the wave of tightening yields, taking advantage of every opportunity that came its way." In addition, the IFR mentioned that what did set apart Portugal from its peripheral peers was the fact that it "managed to monetise the improvements every step of the way" and that "maybe Portugal was not the biggest issuer but it was the one that showed the most spectacular improvement in market access and funding conditions," quoting a banker that had been working with us throughout the entire process.

In following this process, Portugal, like Ireland before us, worked successfully on an alternative to bailouts provided by official creditors. Looking for the support of investors allowed Portugal to recover a higher degree of policy autonomy. The population benefitted from better conditions than the ones that would probably have been allowed by another type of support package, as each government needed to keep their constituencies happy. Keeping a working relationship with investors, based on trust, allowed Portugal to follow a more predictable path and the economy to pursue a nascent recovery. What the investors request to buy bonds and support a country's financing needs is more predictable than negotiating with multiple European countries with different political pressures and cultures. Investors need to see a clear path to debt reduction that will not be at their expense. They are very much focused on the generation of self-sustained growth whereas official support tends to demand sacrifices, austerity, sometimes with a purely demonstrative effect, for political reasons and that can aggravate economic problems instead of solving them. The population may have to pay a higher price. This is why the importance of good market performance became consensual in Portugal in most political circles. Two different governments, with different support basis, but both seem to court market performance and investor participation. We strongly believed that the consequences of a second program, whatever its format, would have been very harmful for the Portuguese population. The economic situation of Portuguese households was very weak and they would not have been able to withstand more austerity measures. This is what happened in Greece and probably made their situation so deep and dramatic, delaying a recovery. The establishment of a strong and wide investor support base, built on mutual trust, becomes an important social asset. Credibility, predictability and constant communication are pillars of this strategy. Portugal is much obliged for the support it received from the markets.

References

1. European Commission, Directorate-General for Economic and Financial Affairs. "Ex Post Evaluation of the Economic Adjustment Programme, Portugal 2011/2014." *Institutional Paper* 40 (November 2016).
2. IGCP. "Note on the EU-IMF Program Exit and Medium-term Fiscal Strategy." (May 14, 2014).
3. Dmitry Gershenson, Albert Jaeger and Subir Lal. "From Crisis to Convergence, Charting a Course for Portugal." International Monetary Fund, European Department (March 2016).
4. Independent Evaluation Office of the International Monetary Fund. "The IMF and the Crisis in Greece, Ireland and Portugal." Evaluation Report. (July 8, 2016).
5. Rolf Strauch, Juan Rojas, Frank O Connor, Cristina Casalinho, Pablo de Ramon-Laca Clausen and Phaedon Kalozois. "Accessing Sovereign Markets – The Recent Experiences of Ireland, Portugal, Spain, and Cyprus." *European Stability Mechanism Working Paper Series*/2 (June 2016).
6. Peter Spiegel and Peter Wise. "Portugal to exit €78bn bailout without emergency backstop," *Financial Times*, (April 30, 2014).
7. Philip Wright. "SSAR Issuer: Republic of Portugal." Review of the Year 2014. International Financing Review, (November 17, 2014).
8. Martin Eichenbaum, Sergio Rebelo and Carlos de Resende. "The Portuguese Crisis and the IMF", *Independent Evaluation Office of the International Monetary Fund* (July 2016).

Index[1]

[1] Note: Page numbers followed by 'n' refer to notes.

J. M. Rato, *The European Debt Crisis*,
https://doi.org/10.1007/978-3-030-61174-3

The manufacturer's authorised representative in the EU is Springer
Nature Customer Service Centre GmbH, Europaplatz 3, 69115 Heidelberg,
Germany. If you have any concerns regarding our products, please
contact ProductSafety@springernature.com

Printed and bound by CPI Group (UK) Ltd, Croydon, CR0 4YY
30/09/2026
02225475-0011